Getting Your
Little Darlings
to Behave

Other parenting books from Continuum

A Parent's Guide to Primary School – Katy Byrne and
Harvey McGavin
Help your Teenager Succeed at School – Michael Papworth
Educating Your Child at Home – Alan Thomas and Jane Lowe

Also by Sue Cowley

Getting the Buggers to Behave: 2nd Edition
Getting the Buggers to Think
Getting the Buggers to Write
Guerilla Guide to Teaching
How to Survive your First Year in Teaching
Sue Cowley's Teaching Clinic

Getting Your Little Darlings to Behave

Sue Cowley

continuum
LONDON • NEW YORK

Continuum
The Tower Building   15 East 26th Street
11 York Road   New York,
London SE1 7NX   NY 10010

British Library Cataloguing-in-Publication Data
A catalogue record for this book is available from the British Library.

ISBN: 0 8264 6502 1 (paperback)

Library of Congress Cataloging-in-Publication Data
A catalogue record for this book is available from the Library of Congress.

Typeset by RefineCatch Limited, Bungay, Suffolk
Printed and bound in Great Britain by MPG Books Ltd, Bodmin, Cornwall

Contents

To Álvie

Acknowledgements

Many thanks go to Anthony Haynes, Suzanne Ashley, Katie Sayers, Christina Parkinson and all the team at Continuum, for all their efforts on my behalf. A very special thank you goes to my editor Alexandra Webster, for her endless patience and many positive comments.

Thanks and love go as always to Tilak, my 'big darling', and also to my mum for being an ever willing grandma/ babysitter.

Thanks to all the mums and babies in my own network of support: especially all the girls at the October 2002 club, and all the ladies at the Friday lunch club. I don't know what I'd do without you!

Finally, a big 'thank you' goes to Elka, who helped me out in my hour of need, and who does a wonderful job of being a parent.

Introduction

Being a parent can and should be great fun. You get the chance to see your child grow up, learning something new every day; you have the opportunity to share your love and your life with your child; you get the chance to rediscover your sense of wonder and excitement as you watch your child finding out about the world. On the other hand, being a parent also brings its fair share of challenges, particularly if you have to deal with difficult behaviour. With this book I hope to help make bringing up your child a fun and positive experience for you, so that you can enjoy the job of being a parent to the full.

When we first become parents, most of us have never done anything even remotely similar before. We might have 'managed' other people in a workplace, but very few of us will have experience in dealing with the challenges that a young child might throw at us. This is why it can be so hard for us to deal with our children's behaviour, and why there is so much for us to learn.

In this book I offer practical and realistic advice for parents about how to manage children's behaviour. As with my books for teachers, it is written in a realistic and down to earth way. I give tips and strategies that will help you deal with all the behaviour issues that you face, from getting the basics right, through to dealing with more serious problems. As a teacher, I've dealt with the behaviour of literally thousands of different children; as a parent I understand just how stressful managing behaviour 24/7 can be. The strategies that

I outline in this book are simple to understand and put into practice, but will make an amazing difference to your children's behaviour.

This book gives a whole range of ideas to help you manage your children's behaviour, focusing particularly on the years between 0 and 11, when many of the patterns for behaviour in later life are being set. I include tips, advice and strategies, as well as a series of exercises for you to complete. The exercises that I give are designed to help you become more aware of your own attitudes to behaviour. I also give you lots of concrete techniques and ideas that you can easily put into practice in your own home. My aim is to offer you realistic advice that will actually work.

The ideas that I give in this book are not difficult to put into place. The hard thing is sticking to them over time. This is particularly difficult when you are feeling tired, stressed or simply in a bad mood. But with persistence and hard work the advice that you find in this book will make your life as a parent a whole lot easier. I'd like to stress right from the very start, though, that none of us are 'perfect' parents. Do try not to be too hard on yourself when you make mistakes, and when you find it difficult or impossible to follow the advice that I give. I know from personal experience just how hard it is to put all the theory into practice!

Coping with difficult behaviour is never easy. As a teacher, I see just how true this is when I'm working with a class that contains disruptive or confrontational students. Of course it's just as true when you are dealing with your own child or children. At least as a teacher I know that my children will be heading home at the end of each day. But as parents we have to deal with our children twenty-four hours a day, seven days a week. There is no escape, even when things get really tough. There is also that overpowering feeling that your children are your responsibility. If you get it wrong, there is no one else to blame.

Managing behaviour well has a lot to do with your attitude. You have the choice of seeing poor behaviour as a problem, one that gives you lots of stress and perhaps some grey hairs too. Alternatively you can view it as a challenge – as a chance to become a better parent and a better person as well. One of the key ideas that I stress in this book is that you should try and stay positive, no matter how hard this is. If you can maintain a positive attitude, you will encourage better behaviour from your children, and you will also deal with difficult behaviour in the most effective way.

You'll notice that throughout this book I try to avoid using the word 'bad' when talking about behaviour. Instead, I prefer to use words such as 'poor', 'difficult' or 'challenging'. You might see this as an example of political correctness gone mad, but it's actually important to make the distinction. You need to learn to see the behaviour as being 'poor', rather than your child as being 'bad'. This will help you in understanding and working with your child when he or she really tests your patience. It will also help you to avoid labelling or prejudging your child. You need to fix in your mind that, when misbehaviour occurs, most of the time this is not because your child is being deliberately difficult. Often he or she simply doesn't understand what poor behaviour is, perhaps because no one has ever explained.

I'd like to end this introduction by wishing you all the best in managing your children's behaviour. Above everything else, it takes hard work, persistence and dedication. But with a lot of time and a lot of effort, you really will succeed in getting your little darling or darlings to behave. And if you can encourage your children to behave in the best possible way, you will be able to enjoy the wonderful job of being a parent!

Sue Cowley
www.suecowley.co.uk

Please note
To keep things simple, I talk about children as 'she' and 'he' in alternate chapters.

When I use the term 'parents' throughout this book, I mean whoever looks after the child. This might be the child's biological parent or parents. Of course it could also mean the child's adoptive or foster parents, a sibling or any other person who cares for the child.

ONE

Getting Started

In this chapter I give you an introduction to the whole subject of behaviour. The ideas that I give here are based on my experience of dealing with the behaviour (and misbehaviour) of literally thousands of different children, both in the classroom and in the home. This chapter will help you understand more about behaviour: both the behaviour you want, and the behaviour that you don't. The information included in this chapter will also help you access the ideas in the rest of the book.

The first part of this chapter looks at some of the reasons why children misbehave. I explore how behaviour (both good and bad) is learned. I talk about why you need to manage behaviour, and give you some initial ideas about how to do this. I also examine some of the things that might go wrong for you when you're dealing with your own children's behaviour.

It's very hard to step back from a child who is misbehaving, and to look at things realistically. This is most difficult when we are dealing with our own children, because we are so close to them and to the situation. The tips and thoughts in this chapter will help you see what happens between you and your children in a clear and rational way.

Why does my child misbehave?

There is *always* a reason for our behaviour, no matter how silly or unimportant it might seem. If we want to change (or keep up) a certain way of behaving, we need to understand why it is happening in the first place. As well as there always being a reason for misbehaviour, there is also always a reason for good behaviour. If we can pinpoint the reasons for right or wrong behaviour, then we can start to change things for the better.

Below are some ideas about why children misbehave. Later on in the book you'll pick up lots of tips about how you can deal with these problems.

Reason one: exploration

Young children have very little understanding about the world in which they live. They don't know what things are, how or why they work, what is dangerous or safe, and so on. Of course, they are very interested to find out, and this can lead to problems! Children get the information they need about their world in a number of different ways. They will learn by:

- testing things out and making mistakes
- what their parents tell them or show them about the world
- the way that their parents react to them when they explore
- the example that their parents set in their own inter-actions with objects, people and places

With young children, what we might see as 'being naughty' is often just the child trying to increase her understanding of the world. For instance, children are often fascinated by shiny objects. Your child might reach up towards a valuable glass vase at her grandparents' house. When she does this, she is not really being naughty. She simply doesn't yet understand how or why it is 'wrong' or unsafe.

Our job as parents is to introduce our children gradually to their world, making sure that they stay safe while they learn.

As they grow older, we can gradually give more trust to our children, handing over the reins of responsibility to them for managing their own behaviour. This book will show you exactly how this can be done.

Reason two: looking for the limits

A natural part of growing up is finding out where the limits are. Children test us all the time, to see how far they can go before an adult says 'stop!'. This is all part of learning the rules of the society and the world in which they live.

For example, at first your baby might drop her cup on the floor to see what you do. After a while she might move on to throwing the cup across the room, again to test your reaction. Later on still she might even resort to chucking the cup at you to see if you are going to allow this behaviour.

Boundary testing continues right throughout childhood. An older child might experiment with using 'naughty words', or swearing, to test out your reactions. We have a vital job as parents in setting the limits or boundaries for our children, so that they learn how to behave 'properly'. You can find lots of information about how to set and stick to boundaries on pages 82–85 of this book.

Reason three: the signals we send

Right from the very earliest days of their lives, our children look at the signals we send to them to help them learn how to behave. We constantly give them messages about appropriate behaviour, hopefully offering them a role model about what is right, and what is not allowed. Bear in mind that you will be sending both positive and negative signals – your aim should be to send more of the positive ones as far as you possibly can! We send signals in a number of different ways, some very obvious, some more subtle:

- how we ourselves behave – with our children, with our families and friends, and with other people
- the way that we talk to and with our children – the words that we use, and the way that we speak
- how we use our bodies to send signals – this includes the way we use our faces and our body language

- the way that we react to positive or negative behaviour

The role model that we provide plays a vital part in sending these signals to our children. A child who is told not to shout at others, but who hears her parents arguing and shouting with each other, will naturally be confused. She will be unsure about what this means for her. Does it mean that she can shout at people as well? Does it mean that only adults can shout? If it does, this will seem very unfair to the child. All the time we need to remember that we are modelling what is right and wrong for our children by the way that we ourselves behave.

Of course, as they grow older, our children will also be influenced by what their friends or classmates do. They will also look at the other adults they meet, for instance the way that their teachers behave towards them. However, the most powerful and constant influence is nearly always that of the parents and the home environment.

Our aim as parents should be to set the model of behaviour that we want our children to follow, to send the right signals as often as we can. Having said all this, do bear in mind that you are bound to slip up, especially when you're tired or in a bad mood. Do try not to be too hard on yourself when this does happen – I make mistakes all the time, and I'm an 'expert' in managing behaviour, with years of experience in this area. Chapter 6 deals in lots of detail with the whole area of sending signals.

Reason four: boredom and attention seeking

Have you ever noticed how, when you take a misbehaving child out of the house, she will often stop messing around? Or how your baby is whingeing for no reason, but when you start to play with her she suddenly stops?

Just like adults, children get bored. They also want our attention. In fact, our attention is one of the biggest rewards that we can give them. The bored child will often start misbehaving to get this attention. Unfortunately, giving a child attention for poor behaviour is one of the biggest mistakes we can make, because it simply reinforces the behaviour that we don't want.

The difficult thing about ignoring attention-seeking

behaviour is that this type of behaviour automatically draws our attention. When I'm teaching a class of students, it's the child who is messing around that will pull my focus. As a teacher, I have to fight very hard against this natural reaction, aiming instead to concentrate on those children who are doing what I want. As parents, we face exactly the same challenge!

Another difficulty in dealing with boredom or attention seeking is that real life has a habit of getting in the way. You might dearly love to sit and play with your child, but it could be that you have a pile of dirty washing and a million other chores to do. You could be more than happy to head out to the shops with your toddler, but it might be that your nine-year-old's favourite TV programme is about to start. In this book you'll learn how to deal with these type of situations in the best possible way, although do bear in mind that sometimes there simply is no easy answer.

Reason five: discomfort and unhappiness

When your child is uncomfortable or upset in some way, you are far more likely to experience difficult behaviour, particularly the classic 'whinge' that drives the best of us to distraction. If your baby is tired, has a dirty nappy or is teething, she will probably cry until you sort things out for her. If your child is hungry, unwell, upset or simply in a bad mood, she is likely to complain until she feels better, or until her needs are met.

Young children have not yet learnt to control their impulses. When they are feeling under the weather or miserable, they can't rationalize this in the same way that we can as adults. (In fact, let's face it, even as adults we are not always entirely successful at keeping our discomfort to ourselves, rather than taking it out on those close to us.)

An adult might be able to say to him or herself 'Okay, I'm in a bad mood but it's not fair to take it out on someone else', or 'Right, I'm feeling a bit peckish but it's nearly dinner time and I really should wait for my meal'. This is much harder for children to do. For the very youngest children, there is a further problem in that they cannot tell us what's going on inside them. It's up to us as the parents to work it out, and we will inevitably get it wrong on occasions.

When it comes to tiredness, do bear in mind that if your child is not rested, then you probably won't be either. If you've been up all night dealing with an upset or sick child, you will be less able to deal with any misbehaviour in the best way, simply because you're stressed and exhausted.

How behaviour is learned

Although our personalities might be hardwired or inbred to a certain extent, no one is actually born behaving in one way or another. Tiny babies react pretty much in a completely instinctive way. In the first few weeks and months they don't have any idea of what is 'right' or 'wrong'. As yet they have no experience of the society in which they live, and the expectations of that society when it comes to their behaviour.

Babies must learn how we expect them to behave through interacting with the people in their lives, and with the big wide world around them. It is only slowly that they learn what behaviour is or is not allowed, and this learning process takes years and years. In fact, even when we are adults we sometimes still behave in the wrong way.

There are lots of different ways in which children learn their behaviour. These include:

■ *Their parents as a role model* Our children spend a lot of time with us, especially when they are very young. Because of this, it's really important to remember that we can show them what good behaviour means. We act as role models for our children. If we have poor or negative habits ourselves, then we shouldn't be surprised if they pick up these habits along the way.

■ *The way we manage our children's behaviour* Our children learn a great deal about good behaviour from the way that we deal with them. This applies especially to the way that we respond when they don't do what we want. They are watching us for clues – if we shout at them, or become confrontational and aggressive, then this is what they will learn about how people relate to each other.

6

- *Other people* As our children grow older, other influences begin to count. Once they start to mix with others, whether at nursery or at school, our children begin to see that people might behave in a different way to their parents. Peer pressure can be a very strong influence on behaviour: either positive or negative. A teenager who mixes with a gang involved in crime will find it very hard not to fit in by taking on the same poor behaviour. Other people can also help our children to learn good behaviour, for instance, teachers and other authority figures.

- *Influences inside and outside the home* Our children also pick up ideas about good and bad behaviour from the media. Television, films, video games, newspapers, and so on will all have some impact on those children who watch or read them. The kind of environment in which our children live might also have an effect on the way that they behave. For instance, a child who lives in a high crime area might be influenced by this fact, although this is by no means a certainty if the parenting is of a good quality. A child who lives in an isolated rural area might turn to bad behaviour out of boredom and frustration, although again the parents can influence this situation for the better.

Why do I need to 'manage' my children's behaviour?

You might feel that you should know how to manage your children's behaviour, that it should be an instinctive and natural thing for you to do. You might believe that you shouldn't need anyone to teach you how to do it. But when we become parents for the first time, most of us have never had to manage anyone else's behaviour before. Even those of you who manage other people in your work will probably not be used to dealing with children, who present a very different challenge. It is for this reason that this book will prove so useful to you.

In today's world very few of us live in extended family groups. This means that we miss out on the wisdom of previous generations. With the advent of technologies such as television, telephones and computers, our children can be influenced in their behaviour by many external factors. The parent of today has to cope with all this and more.

Getting behaviour right is important for a whole range of reasons. I'd like to list some of these here, to persuade you just how important and useful behaviour management techniques could be to you.

- *Creating a positive home life* What we all want, surely, is a calm and controlled situation in our home lives. A place where our children can be brought up in a fun, positive and beneficial way. Positive behaviour management will help you do this, by showing you how to get your little darlings to behave.

- *Developing good relationships* We all love our children, but having a good relationship does not always follow on from this. If your child is testing you by misbehaving, then you will probably find yourself getting irritated with her, and perhaps even disliking her. This is not a good basis for developing a strong relationship between the two of you. But if you can teach your child how to behave properly, you will be able to enjoy the best possible relationship that you can.

- *Academic success* If we bring up our children to behave properly, this will set them up to succeed as they move more and more outside the home. When your child starts school, she will already understand how to behave properly. She will understand what the boundaries of good behaviour are, rather than having to make lots of mistakes and be taught how to behave by her teachers. Her good behaviour will have a very positive effect on her academic success, because she will be able to focus properly on her work right from the earliest days of her education. As a teacher, I can vouch for the fact that those children who do know how to behave well are far more likely to succeed at school.

- *Social success* As well as achieving academic success, the child who knows how to behave appropriately will also get on well with her peers. She will make friends quickly, and hang onto these friends, because she knows how to treat them properly. These social skills will be useful to your child at school, and also beyond in the wider world.

Top tips for managing behaviour

As this point I'd like to give you some 'top tips' for managing behaviour. These initial ideas give you an overview of what you're aiming to achieve. All the strategies that I give below are dealt with in much greater detail later on in this book.

Sue's Top Tips

- *Be positive* Focus as much as possible on what you and your child are doing well.
- *Set up structures and routines* Children like to know where they stand: consistent structures and routines help them to feel more secure.
- *Set the boundaries* Make it clear to your children what is, and is not, allowed.
- *Be consistent* Try to keep your requirements and approaches the same at all times.
- *Make behaviour a choice* Give your child responsibility for her behaviour, getting her to accept the consequences of behaving in the wrong way.
- *Start 'training' as early as possible* Right from the word 'go', manage your child's behaviour in a positive and assertive way.
- *Use the 'carrot' over the 'stick'* Rewards will always work much better than sanctions in getting the good behaviour that you want.
- *Be reasonable, but don't reason with them* Don't get drawn into pointless arguments or discussions – set fair limits and stick to them like glue.
- *Be flexible* Managing behaviour is not about 'win or lose' – sometimes you will need to bend a little to get it right.

What doesn't work

As well as understanding what does work when it comes to managing behaviour, it's also vital to understand what doesn't work. At this point in the book I'd like to offer you a list of the 'worst sins': the negative things that you need to avoid doing at all costs, the ways that you might deal with behaviour which are just going to make the situation worse. Do accept, though, that there will be times when you slip into bad habits or when you are simply too tired to get it right.

Sue's 'Worst Sins'

- *The empty threat* Try never to threaten a punishment that you're not going to use: this only weakens your position in the future.
- *Getting wound up* It's all too easy to lose your rag when your child is messing you around, but anger is simply not an effective control strategy.
- *Being negative* Sometimes it's hard to stay positive, but a negative approach will only make things worse.
- *Being confrontational* When faced with a confrontational or obstinate child, aim to stay calm rather than taking an equally aggressive attitude.
- *Getting drawn in* Getting pulled into arguments is a waste of your energy – if you set fair boundaries, you don't need to debate them.
- *Backing them into a corner* Children don't understand how or when to back down: learn to be flexible when necessary, and give your child a 'way out'.
- *Beating yourself up* Be positive with yourself, as well as with your child: we all make mistakes, it's the ability to learn from them that counts.

TWO

Your Parenting Style

None of us is born knowing how to behave: it's up to us to teach our children right from wrong, to show them what we believe to be good behaviour. One of the difficulties we face is deciding what we actually mean by 'good behaviour'. This will be different for every single person reading this book. You might take a very strict approach with your children, you could take a very free and flexible one. In fact, many of us will fall somewhere in between these two styles.

Over the years as a teacher, I've had the chance to experiment with a whole range of different styles when it comes to managing behaviour. As I gained in experience, I came to see that some approaches are more useful and effective than others. In this book I aim to let you in on some of the ideas and strategies that I've learnt.

In this chapter you'll find lots of thoughts and ideas about parenting styles, and you'll get a chance to think about what sort of parent you are, or want to be. This will help you to understand the best approaches and strategies for you to use when managing behaviour. It will also help you change your style as needed to improve your relationship with your children.

As part of thinking about our parenting styles, I look at the role that our emotions play in our style as a parent. I deal with the ways in which parents can act as a team to ensure the best behaviour from their children, and at how you might work alongside any other people who care for your child. Finally, I look briefly at the up and downsides of being a single parent.

What sort of parent are you?

We all use different styles as parents, because we are all individuals who do things in our own ways. Understanding what sort of parent you are is important when it comes to working out which strategies will work best for you. The style that you choose to bring up your children will vary for a number of different reasons. These reasons include:

- *Your upbringing* Most of us are strongly influenced by the way we ourselves were brought up. It could be that you had very positive experiences as a child. If this is the case, you might decide to follow in your parents' footsteps when it comes to managing your own children's behaviour. It could be that you felt your childhood was too strict or too free. If you didn't agree with the way your parents brought you up then you might try to do the opposite with your own child.

- *The type of person you are* The way that you manage your children will also depend on the sort of person you are. If you're small and timid, you probably won't use a style that needs a loud voice or a confident manner. If you're someone who likes life to be very structured and controlled, you are unlikely to bring up your children in a free and relaxed way.

- *The type of children you have* You will hopefully vary your parenting style to the suit the type of children you have. Every child is a unique individual, and this applies just as much to the way they behave as to every other aspect of their lives. For instance, we would use a different style for a quiet and shy child, and a loud and confident one. Of course in a large family you might face a situation where you have several different types of children to deal with, and this will stretch your parenting skills to the limit.

■ *Your environment and your personal situation* Our environment does play a part in the way that we manage behaviour, and the strategies that we might use. These strategies are not necessarily any better or worse, they are just different. For instance, there will be differences in managing your children if you have to raise them in a tiny city flat, without any outside space, as opposed to a huge mansion in the countryside. Similarly, if you are a single parent, this will impact on the way you manage behaviour, simply because there is only one of you available to deal with your child.

Types of parenting style

In this section I look at the three main 'types' of parenting style. The descriptions that I give below are based on the three most common styles of managing behaviour: from a strict, highly structured and authoritarian approach, to a very liberal and relaxed one. As you will see, the two ends of the scale – 'Strict and severe' and 'Loose and liberal' are extreme examples of particular parenting approaches, designed hopefully to be interesting and thought provoking. You may well tend towards one end of the scale, but probably not to quite the extent given below.

In real life, most of us will take a position that is fairly close to the middle of the three styles, adopting aspects of each type to make up our own approach. In fact, my years of experience in managing behaviour have shown me that this 'Firm but fair' style offers the best way of working with children. You, of course, will have your own opinions about how strict or liberal you need or want to be. The key is finding the style that works best for both you and your children.

For each of the parenting types, I give an outline of the typical opinions, attitudes and approaches involved. I also look at some of the upsides and downsides associated with each particular style. As you look at the description of the different types you might like to:

- think about where you are currently in relation to these outlines
- look at the list of potential difficulties associated with each style, and think about whether you currently experience any of these problems
- consider whether the issues you face with your children might be connected to your style of managing behaviour
- think about how you could adapt your style, perhaps becoming slightly stricter or a little more liberal as necessary

Of course in many homes there will be two parents managing behaviour together. It could be that one of you leans more towards the authoritarian end of the scale, and one of you towards the more liberal style. Similarly, in a home with a number of children, whose temperaments differ, it could be that you also need to adopt slightly different styles with each child.

Style One: Strict and severe

This style is what we might call old-fashioned or 'Victorian'. It involves a very rigid and structured approach to parenting, where children are expected to do as they are told, without question.

Typical opinions
- a strict and rigid routine is the best thing for a child
- children these days have too much freedom
- behaviour is much worse than it used to be
- children should be seen and not heard
- children need to be taught to respect their elders

Typical attitudes
- my child behaves much better than other people's children
- other people are too liberal with their children's behaviour

- there's too much emphasis on asking children what they want – it's up to the adult to decide for them
- smacking children for misbehaviour is an excellent method of discipline

Typical approaches
- rigid routines for the child's day
- very little flexibility allowed in these routines
- dealing with misbehaviour by applying strict sanctions
- use of smacking for control
- focus on structured learning rather than imaginative playing
- shouting as a sanction for misbehaviour

Upsides of this style
- the clear routine means the child knows where he stands
- a structured environment gives the child a feeling of security
- this type of parent is normally very clear about his or her expectations
- the child will probably find it easy to fit into the 'school rules' when he starts at school

Downsides of this style
- with a rigid approach, parents can back a misbehaving child into a corner
- this can tend to lead to a lot of confrontations
- highly structured routines leave little room for flexibility and the unexpected
- as the child grows older, he may start to fight against these approaches
- over use of strict sanctions, such as smacking, can leave the parent with 'nowhere to go' when something really serious happens

Style Two: Firm but fair

This is my preferred style – the one I try to adopt as often as possible, and the one for which I would advise you to aim. This style strikes a good balance between the structure needed for clear expectations, and the flexibility required for dealing with real-life situations.

Typical opinions
- a clear and structured routine is very good for children
- parents need to apply some flexibility in managing their children's behaviour
- children should have at least some say in what they can and can't do
- I'm the adult – I usually know what's best for my child, and I set clear boundaries to show where the limits are

Typical attitudes
- my child needs to know where he stands when it comes to behaviour
- I know how I want my child to behave, but I don't always get it right
- I can empathize with the problems that other people have with their children
- I try not to smack or shout at my child, but I understand why it happens
- children need to be brought up in a positive and loving environment

Typical approaches
- clearly structured routines for the child's day, but flexible when needed
- use of positive approaches and rewards whenever possible – making good behaviour the right and attractive choice
- turning to sanctions as a 'last resort' – avoiding smacking and shouting
- a clear understanding of what is required, and a refusal to get involved in pointless discussions

Upsides of this style
- the child feels a sense of involvement in managing his own behaviour
- clear expectations mean that the child knows what he should do
- flexibility is available when needed – routines can be adapted at short notice
- this type of parent normally has a very good relationship with the child

Downsides of this style
- it can be hard to find and maintain that balance between clarity and flexibility
- if the parent is too 'firm', the downsides of the 'strict and severe' style can come into play
- similarly if the parent is too 'fair', the downsides of the 'loose and liberal' style might apply

Style Three: Loose and liberal

This style of parenting is very much a result of modern attitudes to children. I'm all in favour of the belief that children should have a say in their lives as far as possible. The issue is whether an overly liberal style means that we don't give our children the structure and limits that they need.

Typical opinions
- our children have a right to decide how they behave
- you're only young once – too many rules dampen a child's spirit
- parents don't necessarily know what's best for their children
- I like to be adaptable and flexible, and that includes the way I manage behaviour

Typical attitudes
- all children need is their parents' love – they'll learn how to behave in their own good time
- I discuss with my child how he should behave – it's not up to me to tell him
- creativity and imagination are the most important things for a child
- smacking and shouting are totally wrong and an abuse of a parent's position

Typical approaches
- little routine in the child's day, a flexible and some-times chaotic approach
- use of positive approaches and rewards – avoiding sanctions at all costs
- never using smacking or shouting as control strategies
- lots of imaginative play and messy creative activities
- discussing misbehaviour at great length when it happens

Upsides of this style
- the child is asked to learn how to manage his own behaviour
- there is great flexibility when the unexpected occurs
- there is unlikely to be much confrontation between parent and child
- there is typically a strong feeling of love and creativity in the home
- relationships between parent and child are normally very positive and close

Downsides of this style
- the child is not clear about what is and is not allowed
- as a result, a lot of boundary testing will probably occur
- the unwillingness to use sanctions can mean that the child 'gets away' with lots of minor misbehaviour
- the lack of routines can lead to a chaotic and over-excitable atmosphere
- the child might find difficulty in fitting into a more structured environment, such as school

What sort of relationship do you want?

When you're looking at your own parenting style, it is worth taking some time to think about the type of relationship that you want to develop with your children. If you can establish how you want your children to see you, this will help you understand which strategies in this book will work best for you. You will also see what changes, if any, you need to make to your parenting style. An important part of deciding on the parent/child relationship, is working out your own priorities. None of us have endless reserves of time, and we need to make decisions about what we see as most important within our relationship.

Here's an exercise that will help you establish the type of relationship you want with your child, and how you can go about achieving it. Look first at the two lists of words below, which describe the way that your children see you, and the type of relationship that you want with them. Think about which of these words best fit with your own ideas about the relationship you have. You will probably notice that these words connect closely to the different types of parenting styles discussed in the section above.

After you've looked at these two lists, go through the list of priorities, considering which points you view as most important, and which can be put lower down the list. This should help you to decide what you most want to achieve in your relationship with your children (and with your partner), and what will have to be given less focus and time. Completing this exercise will hopefully help you maintain a sense of perspective about what you can realistically achieve as a parent.

How do my children see me?

friend
authority figure
disciplinarian
teacher
partner
carer

equal
boss

What sort of relationship do I want with my children?

close
emotional
distant
loving
caring
strict
free
controlled

What are my priorities?

- reading with my children, and helping them to learn
- making time to play and have fun with my children
- keeping a sense of order and calm in my home
- giving my children a feeling of love and security
- getting my children to behave as well as possible
- giving each of my children equal time and attention
- my children's academic success
- my children's emotional development and happiness
- making time and space for myself
- taking the time to maintain my relationship with my partner
- going on exciting and stimulating trips and holidays
- keeping the house clean and tidy
- cooking interesting and nutritional meals
- keeping on top of the washing and ironing

Behaviour and your emotions

Our emotions can get in the way of us making the best response when misbehaviour does occur. Whenever some-one behaves wrongly towards you, whether this is a fellow worker in the office or your child at home, it is almost inevitable that you will react emotionally. But if you allow your emotions to take control you won't be able to deal with any problems in the best way.

Here's an exercise for you to do, to help you think about your own emotions when your child misbehaves. The idea of this exercise is to get you thinking about your emotional reactions to misbehaviour.

1. Read the following scenarios. As you read, think about how you would feel in each of the situations described.

> **Scenario One** You're at home with your child. You've just done the washing and it's sitting in the laundry basket waiting to be put away. You go to answer the phone, and when you get back you discover that the washing has been strewn across the floor.

> **Scenario Two** You go to visit a friend who has a child of a similar age to your own. The children are playing with an expensive toy when an argument starts. Your child hits his friend over the head with the toy, breaking it.

> **Scenario Three** You have spent hours preparing a beautiful meal for your child. When you sit down to eat, he completely refuses to take even a single mouthful of the food. When you try to force him, he picks up his plate and throws it across the room.

2. Now look at the list of words below. These words describe how you might feel in these situations. Consider which of these words best fit with the emotions that you would experience in each of the scenarios.

angry	furious
embarrassed	ashamed
irritated	wound up
annoyed	unhappy
upset	sad
worried	frustrated
anxious	hurt

3. Next, take some time to consider why you feel like this when your child misbehaves. Do any of the following statements sum up what you're feeling?

■ *Scenario One* I've spent ages doing the washing, and now it's on the floor and it's all dirty. I've told him before not to do this, but he just doesn't listen. Can't I even go to answer the phone without him messing me around?

■ *Scenario Two* How embarrassing – my friend must think I've got no control over my own child. I've told him a hundred times before not to hit other children, why does he still do it? The worst thing is that it's such an expensive toy! Now I'm going to have to pay a fortune to replace it.

■ *Scenario Three* I spent hours making that dinner – why won't the little sod eat it? He's doing it on purpose – he knows how long it took me. I'm going to make him eat it, that'll teach him. How dare he throw his plate! Now he's in big trouble.

4. Now think carefully about why the child might be behaving like this in each of these situations, and what might be going on inside his head. Sometimes we need to take a jump in our thoughts to see things from a completely different angle. It's actually very rare that our children misbehave deliberately to hurt or upset us, although it often feels like they do!

Of course, I'm not saying that you shouldn't do anything when misbehaviour does occur. What I am saying is that it can be worthwhile looking at things from your child's perspective to try to understand why he does what he does. Here are some suggestions as to what your child's thought processes could be:

- *Scenario One* Oh look, a big pile of clothes. Why don't I help mummy by trying to put them away? Whoops, I'm not very good at this yet, am I? Oh dear, mummy's not looking very happy with me. Now she's started to shout.

- *Scenario Two* I want that toy! Why won't my friend let me have a go, I always let him play with my stuff when he comes to my house? It's not fair! Oh no, I didn't mean to break it. Now daddy's going to be really cross.

- *Scenario Three* What's this dinner that mummy's made for me? I don't like the look of this at all – I've told her before that I don't like gravy all over my food, but she doesn't listen. Now she's trying to force me to eat it, but it's making me feel sick. There's only one way I can stop her – if I chuck it on the floor she can't make me eat it.

5. Finally, think about how you could react differently in these situations. Imagine yourself staying as cool and calm as possible, and not letting your heart rule the day. What would you do and say? How could you deal with these problems in a calm and unemotional way?

Dealing with your emotions

As a teacher, I try very hard not to let my emotions interfere in my classroom. This is not because I don't care about my children. It's because I know that if I get too emotional I won't be able to handle difficult situations as well as I might. In addition, as a teacher if you allow poor behaviour to get to you, it's unlikely that you'll stay in the job very long. Teachers who work in 'challenging' schools might face children swearing at them, or abusing them, on a daily basis. This becomes impossible to take over a long period of time if you allow it to hurt you.

Here are three of my top tips for handling your emotions. These ideas are ones that I have developed over years of working as a teacher. As a parent, I also try my hardest to put these approaches into practice, but I'm well aware of how difficult it is to actually follow these ideas through.

■ *React with your head, not your heart* As you'll have seen from doing the exercise above, becoming emotional can interfere with the best response to misbehaviour. Our first response when someone behaves badly towards us is inevitably an emotional one. If a child is aggressive or abusive, it is all too easy to react from your heart, and you end up feeling upset or getting defensive. Unfortunately, this is not the best response when it comes to dealing with the child's behaviour in the most effective way. Instead of allowing your heart to rule your reactions, try instead to respond with your head, and to cope with the situation in an intellectual, rational manner.

■ *Stay cool and calm* When they do misbehave, our children are very good at reading our responses. The way that you react will teach them a thing or two about you as a person. Bear in mind that they will also be looking at your reaction as a model of how to behave. If you become angry and worked up, this gives your child an incentive to misbehave in the future. It's also a poor example of behaviour, that you don't want your child to repeat. If you can stay cool and calm instead, the child has less reason to repeat the same behaviour again. A cool response will also start to teach your child about the appropriate way to behave.

■ *Walk away* Sometimes the best thing we can do for ourselves and for our children is simply to walk away. This applies particularly to those situations where the child is refusing point blank to cooperate, or where we are in danger of losing control of ourselves. If you do feel that you cannot cope rationally with what's happening, then make sure your child is safe and take yourself somewhere else so that both of you can calm down.

Parenting as a team

There are often a number of people involved in bringing up a child, whether this is mum and dad, parents and grandparents, parents and childminder or nanny, parents and nursery or school staff, and so on. Once your child starts school, being able to work as a team will be vital in the continued management of your child's behaviour (see Chapter 9 for lots of information about this area).

Of course, when there are two or more of you working with the child, this brings complications of its own when it comes to managing your child's behaviour. The members of the 'team' are more than likely to have different opinions when it comes to how strict or how free it is best to be in managing children's behaviour. This can lead to your child receiving mixed messages: mum says he can do something, but dad says he can't; his parents say it's okay to behave in a certain way, but his grandparents are shocked and horrified by the same behaviour; his parents allowed him to do 'x' at home, but it's totally against the school rules.

You could find that your child starts to take advantage of this, playing one adult off against the other and confusing the issue of what behaviour you actually want and expect. The tips and ideas below cover both working as a parenting team, and also working together with other adults in managing your child's behaviour.

- *Take care of your relationship* The arrival of a baby inevitably brings a lot of upheaval to a household. Where before there were just the two of you, now there is another human being who is entirely reliant on you both. It can be hard to find time to maintain your relationship when you have a baby to take care of, but it is vital to make time for each other. If you and your partner start to take things out on each other, then this will have a negative impact on the way that you deal with your child's behaviour. Putting aside time to spend as a couple is a vital part of parenting as a team. This applies even more to families with a number of children. Although it will be very hard to make space for yourselves with so many demands on your time, it really is vital for developing and maintaining a strong parenting team.

- *See it as a partnership* When two or more adults are working together to manage behaviour, it's important to develop a sense of partnership. It's not a case of parents or carers against the child, but rather the adults working together with the child to get things right. Having a sense of working together will also help you to avoid the inevitable quarrels that might arise when you have to

25

decide what is and isn't allowed. You'll find lots of ideas for creating a strong home/school partnership in Chapter 9.

■ *Enlist the help of your wider 'team'* If you have more than one child in your household, then your team will include all the members of your family. It is well worth asking older children to help out with the younger siblings, and explaining to them exactly how they can best assist you. Of course, you must reward them for their help, to encourage them. This reward might be as simple as saying 'thanks for being so grown-up about helping me out'.

■ *Use behaviour management methods* The methods that I discuss in this book are not just applicable to children – they also work extremely well with adults. If you are having difficulties in working as a team with the other carers in your child's life, then why not put some of the strategies from this book into practice? For instance, one of the key ideas in this book is that positive approaches are always more effective than negative ones. Bearing this in mind, you might praise your mother-in-law for how wonderfully she brought up her son/your husband. You could then go on to ask her to prove how flexible and adaptable she is by trying out some of the more 'new-fangled' approaches in that book by Sue Cowley that you've just read. This is far more likely to have the required effect, than simply saying 'This is what I want you to do and you must do it.'

■ *Have team expectations* With a number of different behaviour managers, it really is important to try and decide on your expectations together, otherwise confusions will arise. Once your expectations have been established, you must try to keep them as similar as you can at all times. What you want to avoid is the situation where a child does one thing and mum says 'no!', whereas when he does the same thing dad or grandma says 'that's okay'. Your aim at all times must be to work towards the same expectations of your child. Of course, this is relatively easy when you are working with your partner, or when you are paying for childcare. It is far more difficult when the other carer is a family member, perhaps someone from a different generation, with different expectations of what is 'best' for your child. My best advice would be to explain to your team of carers exactly why team expectations are so important. The list below pinpoints three of the key ideas:

- if the adults' expectations of behaviour are different, it is completely confusing for the child, who doesn't know which model of behaviour to follow
- having different expectations weakens the position of the individual adult when it comes to asking for what you want
- it gives your child the opportunity to play you off against each other, by saying 'daddy/nanny lets me do this'

Good cop/bad cop

Many parents decide to use a 'good cop/bad cop' approach when it comes to dealing with their children. In fact, this style of parenting will often develop naturally, simply because of your differing personalities. With the 'good cop/ bad cop' approach, one parent acts as the disciplinarian, while the other takes on a more comforting and gentle role. The disciplinarian has traditionally been the father who goes out to work, with the threat of 'when your father comes home he will . . .' being used to encourage good behaviour. Of course, this is changing as many women also choose to go out to work.

There are both advantages and disadvantages to using this approach, although I would tend to argue that there are more downsides than upsides. I list some of the potential advantages and disadvantages below. It is of course up to you to make up your own mind about whether this particular parenting style will work for you.

Advantages

- this approach can fit well with two different personalities or parenting styles
- it offers you a good way of deferring sanctions (see p. 125 for an explanation of this term)
- the 'bad cop' can be an effective sanction

27

Disadvantages

- deferring the role of punisher to one parent can weaken the 'good cop's' position when it comes to asking for specific behaviours
- the child might start to turn to the 'good cop' to get what he wants
- this approach can lead to inconsistencies in your expectations
- the roles will need to be consistently maintained for this approach to work
- it can also lead to tensions between the parents, as you might feel resentful about having to continue to play the role you have set for yourself
- the 'bad cop' might have less of a close relationship with the child

Parenting on your own

As I said at the start of this book, being a parent is not easy. This perhaps applies especially to those people who are single parents. In this section I look briefly at the downsides of parenting on your own. If you can learn to acknowledge these difficulties, you will help yourself to keep a perspective about just how much you are achieving. I also list some of the potential advantages of working on your own, hopefully to encourage you to look for the positives in your situation.

The downsides

- there is only ever one of you to look after your child or children, and to deal with behaviour issues
- the feeling that you cannot 'escape' the responsibility of looking after your child, even for a few minutes, can be very wearing on you as a person
- you might worry that your children lack a role model: either a male role model if you are a single mum, or a female model if you are a single dad
- as a single parent you will have to learn to take on both roles when it comes to bringing up your child

- you might be in a situation where you have broken up with the other parent only once your child is older. This could cause problems with your child's behaviour because he is upset or confused about the split

The upsides

- it is much easier to be consistent when there is only one of you
- you get to make all the choices about expectations, and to decide exactly how your children will be brought up
- there is no one for your child to appeal to – what you say goes
- taking on both roles will force you to develop your skills in dealing with behaviour
- you might find that your child becomes more responsible at an earlier age, simply because he must

THREE

The Seven
Cs

In this chapter I'm going to look at what I call the seven Cs. These are seven words that, for me, sum up the attitude and approach that you need to take to get good behaviour from your children. As a parent, you are responsible for teaching your children how to behave, and you must set a good example for them as often as you possibly can. The seven Cs offer you ways of encouraging positive behaviour, and also of dealing with negative behaviour in the best way. When it comes down to it good behaviour management has a lot to do with getting your attitude right.

The ideas that I give here are gathered from years of working with children, both in a school setting and in the home. Although the ideas that I give are easy to understand, they are not so easy to put into practice. You are likely to make a lot of mistakes along the way. Having said that, with time and a good deal of effort, the seven Cs will help you to make a difference. And with a positive and confident attitude to dealing with your children's behaviour, you will set them up for a successful and well-behaved future.

The seven Cs

Certain
Confident
Consistent
Calm
Caring
Careful
Creative

Certain

The first C stands for 'certain'

What our children need is for their parents to be absolutely, completely certain about what it is we want from them. If we can offer this certainty, it gives them a wonderful feeling of security. They know exactly how we want them to behave, and by repeating what we want again and again, we help them to understand this. We demonstrate to them what we see as appropriate behaviour, and what we believe to be right and wrong.

Being certain is actually much harder than you might think. There are some issues where what we want will be obvious – for instance if your child is banging a china plate against a glass table, you clearly want her to stop immediately. However, you will also have to make decisions about areas of behaviour that are much more personal and individual. For example, how much television can she watch, what types of food can she eat, which words do you count as 'swearing', and so on? The responsibility for making these decisions lies with us as parents, particularly when our children are too young to make their own choices.

Here are some ideas and tips to help you be as certain as you can with your own children:

- *Work out what you do and don't want* As I pointed out above, you might think that knowing what you want is very simple. In fact it's surprisingly difficult to be completely definite and certain about what you expect from your children. You've probably got some vague idea in your mind about what you see as 'good' or 'correct' behaviour, and what you believe to be 'bad' or 'incorrect'. But when it comes down to actually defining how you want your children to behave, it is hard to be completely sure. It really does pay to take some time to be absolutely certain about what exactly you yourself want, so that you can put this across to your children in a clear and simple way.

- *Define your personal expectations* In teaching, we call this idea of being certain knowing your 'expectations'. Every good teacher will have very clear expectations of his or her class when it comes to their behaviour. You might be hoping that I will write down a list of expectations for you to follow, but the thing about expectations is that they will be different for every single one of us. Some of us will have very strict expectations of our children's behaviour, others will allow their children to be more free in the way that they behave. You need to work out what your own personal expectations are, and then stick to them like glue!

- *Aim high* It is often the case that the higher expectations you have of your children, the better they will behave, and the more likely they will be to live up to what you want. Children do love to please the adults in their lives, so set the standards high and make them aim for the very best. In Chapter 5 (pp. 75–79) you can find lots of information about expectations. I look at what the term means, how to work out what your own expectations are, and so on.

- *Let your children in on the secret* As well as knowing yourself what you want, you must also demonstrate this to your children. Never assume that they will just know – they will have to be told or shown, at least once and probably on numerous occasions, until they get the message. Make

32

it 100 per cent clear exactly what you want, and this will help your child understand how she is meant to behave. With very young children who don't yet understand enough language, you will have to show what you want by your actions, rather than your words.

■ *Give a consistent response* I talk a bit further on in this chapter about the importance of consistency. Once you're clear about what you want, and you've shared this with your child, do make sure that you respond in the same way every time the same misbehaviour (or good behaviour) happens. You should aim to ensure that x behaviour always leads to y response. For instance, every time your child hits her little sister, you might put her in her room for a set period of time. This repetition helps her learn that the behaviour is wrong, and also to understand what the consequences of her actions will be.

■ *State what you want* When things do go wrong, and your child misbehaves, you need to state very clearly and calmly exactly what you do want. If your child is old enough to understand, it's also worth talking briefly about why the behaviour is unacceptable. Make it very clear what you want, and tell the child what will happen if the misbehaviour stops (or if necessary what will happen if it continues). Taking this approach will help stop you from resorting to nagging or shouting at your child, an approach which tends not to be very effective. It will force you to be very specific about your requirements and your expectations, and it will also hopefully help you to stay calm and cool.

Although this approach won't give you instant results, if you can stick with it again and again, eventually the message will sink in. So it is that you might say:

■ *'I want you to stop x behaviour right now, please.'*

■ *'You need to stop doing that because it is dangerous/silly/ messy.'*

■ *'If you stop doing that right away, the result will be x.'* or

■ *'If you don't stop doing that right away, the result will be x.'*

■ *Try being surprised, rather than angry* Another very effective approach, when a child is not living up to your expectations, is to react with surprise rather than anger. The thinking behind this is that you are expecting your child to do the very best, and when she doesn't live up to your expectations this disappoints you. So it is that you might respond to misbehaviour by saying in a surprised voice *'I can't believe you're doing that, you were so well behaved this morning when you helped get your baby brother dressed.'*

- *Use 'I want' statements* Your aim should be to tell your children what you want them to do, rather than asking them. This helps you appear very certain about your requirements. Because you are so clear about what you want, your children will pick up on your attitude, and hopefully realize that complying is the best option. Once you have stated what you want, you can then tell the child what the result will be if she complies. Try to tell her what good things will happen if she does as you say, rather than what bad things might happen if she does not. A reward is always more tempting than a sanction. If possible, aim to use these 'I want' statements for positive behaviours, as in the examples below. Here are two suggestions for 'I want' statements, along with some possible consequences:

  - *'I want you to stop flicking your food immediately. If you do I'll let you have some of this delicious pudding.'*

  - *'I want you to help me do the washing up. If you do I'll let you watch television for an extra half an hour tonight.'*

- *Focus on the positive* It's very easy to be clear about what we don't want, but as I've emphasized throughout this section, it's better to focus on what you do want instead. Don't forget to make it clear to your children that good behaviour will lead to rewards, as well as bad behaviour leading to punishment. Do try to praise more often than you punish, because positive methods always work best when dealing with behaviour, although of course I accept there will also be a need for punishment. Sometimes you can distract a child from misbehaviour by suggesting a positive alternative; on other occasions you might feel that it's important actually to address the misbehaviour that has occurred.

Confident

The second C stands for 'confident'

Being confident is very important when it comes to getting your little darlings to behave. Parents who are confident about what they want will communicate a feeling of certainty to their children. If your children see that you mean business, there is less room for them to mess you around: they will eventually realize that it is better just to do what you ask.

It's surprising how strongly your inner feelings can be communicated to your children. You can find lots of information about the ways that you can send signals in Chapter 6. If you become confident about dealing with behaviour, it will also make you feel better about yourself as a parent. Bear in mind that you don't necessarily have actually to feel confident inside, you just need to appear confident on the outside.

Here are some tips for ways that you can help yourself appear confident, and maintain that confident appearance when things get difficult.

- *Make your expectations clear* It's vital to be clear about what you want, and to share this information with your children: this point is worth repeating over and over again, because it's so important.

- *Be firm, but fair* When you do make a request of your child, make sure that what you're asking is fair. Be firm about what you want, and as long as it is reasonable then there will usually be no reason why you should not get what you've requested.

- *Learn how to communicate with your body* Your confidence as a behaviour manager will be communicated by all the signals that you send to your children, particularly through your facial expressions and body language. We all instinctively (and often subconsciously) 'read' other people through the way that they stand, the way they use their faces, and so on. Aim to transmit a confident exterior, even when inside you're a mass of contradictions. Chapter 6 deals with this fascinating area in lots of detail.

- *Get on with it* If what you are asking is fair enough, then it often pays just to get on with it in a confident manner. As long as your requests are justified, then remember that you are the adult, you know what is best, and sticking to what you want will mean doing the best for your child. For instance, if you are just about to finish cooking dinner, and your child has had a reasonable lunch, then there is no reason why she should have a snack and spoil her appetite. As your children get older, you will probably find it much easier to be firm about areas such as this.

- *Know what's good for them* If you've done all you need to as a parent, then you're not doing your child any favours if you indulge her every whim. Our children have to learn that sometimes what you say goes, and that your reasonable requests should not be questioned. Sometimes we all have to do things that we don't necessarily want to do, and this includes our children.

- *Don't give in at the first hurdle* When you set up an expectation, it's really important that you don't fall at the first hurdle. I know how hard this is to do – sometimes the temptation will be overwhelming to just give in for the sake of a quiet life. The problem is, every time you give in you demonstrate a lack of confidence in your expectations. The key is to underline the message that you know what you want and you mean to get it.

Consistent

The third C stands for 'consistent'

Being consistent is easy to say, but very hard to do. A consistent parent will try to keep his or her expectations clear, and always greet the same behaviour with the same reaction. For instance, your child is out in the garden playing, and she throws a stone at her little sister. Your consistent response to this is that it does not match with your expectations of her behaviour. As a sanction, you might take her inside and put her in her room. If you do this every single time she repeats the misbehaviour, she will soon make the connection between what she has done and the punishment for doing it.

This particular sanction works in various ways. Firstly, it makes your expectation of good behaviour perfectly clear. It also communicates the message that if she can't play properly outside, then she will not be allowed to stay out there. Finally, it tells her that the reaction to hurting her sister is to lose your attention. The message you are sending is that if she cannot behave properly, she will have to take the consequences.

Being consistent is very hard to maintain. Often, it might seem easier simply to 'give in' to your children. This is particularly so when you are tired, stressed or just wanting a quiet life. However, every time you give in, and allow your children to do something that doesn't match with your previous expectations, you are storing up trouble for the future.

The two sections below will help you understand more about being consistent. I look first at why being consistent is so important, and then at some ways you can actually achieve this consistency with your child.

Being consistent: why is it so important?

- *Yes/no behaviours* All the time our children are learning about yes/no behaviours. What this means is behaviours that are allowed or welcomed, and those that are not allowed. When we are faced with different types of behaviour, we need to make it perfectly clear which ones are acceptable, or 'yes' behaviours, and which ones are not – the 'no' behaviours. It's tempting sometimes to let it ride when your child does something just a little bit naughty. However, this simply confuses the issue – it's better to be consistent as far as you possibly can.

- *Avoiding confusion* If on one occasion we allow a particular behaviour, then the next time we don't allow it, this confuses the child. She doesn't understand what we want, because we are sending confusing signals. The child will have to keep trying out the misbehaviour until she can establish whether or not it's allowed. The sooner we can make it clear what is and isn't allowed, the better it actually is for our children.

- *Giving security* Being consistent also helps to give your children security. They start to understand that if they do something, mum or dad will always respond in the same way. In their heads, they start to work it out: 'If I do this, mum will be pleased; if I do this, she will be angry.' This helps them see a pattern to their behaviour and also to their lives.

Being consistent: how do I do it?

One of the reasons why good behaviour management is so hard is that we have to try and fight against some of our most natural and instinctive reactions. It's all very well for me to advise you to be consistent, but sometimes you will be tired, hung over, in a bad mood and so on. It's very hard to maintain the right responses when you don't feel in the mood. Don't be afraid to apologize when you do get it wrong – there's no harm in showing that you're human!

However, for behaviour management to work most effectively, it is important that the same behaviour from the child does usually lead to the same response from the parent. Your aim must be to try and overcome your initial reactions. Here are some tips about how you can do this.

- *Fight your first reaction* When your child does misbehave, fight against your first reaction, which might be anger or irritation. You will not be able to offer a consistent response if you are in a bad mood yourself.

- *Deal with you first, the child second* Take a moment to calm yourself down before you wade in to deal with your child. Learn to respond to the behaviour from your head, rather than your heart. What this means is to look at the situation intellectually and rationally, instead of allowing your emotions to rule.

- *Stick to your guns* Sometimes we start down a road with our children, and get tempted to turn back. No matter how tempting it is to give in and change your mind when your child cries or throws a tantrum, do try not to. The problem is that this simply confuses the child, and means it will take longer for her to understand what you want. It's always much better to stick to what you've decided once you get started.

- *Try not to change your mind* One of the problems when we

haven't previously decided on our expectations, is that we make it up as we go along. For instance, you decide that you are going to put your foot down and not let Amy say 'bum' anymore. However, when faced with this problem on a number of previous occasions you have just 'let it go'. This will be difficult for Amy to understand. She has been receiving one message – that it's okay to say 'bum', and now you're telling her the complete opposite. If you do want to change tack halfway about a behaviour that you previously allowed, you need to let the child know what's going on. Here's how you might do this:

- Sit the child down and explain the new rule.

- Make it a positive challenge for the child, for instance saying 'now that you're older, and you can behave so much better, I'm going to stop you doing this.'

- Keep reinforcing the new expectation, but don't expect instant results. Let the child have a little leeway until she fully understands your new wishes.

Calm

The fourth C stands for 'calm'

As I pointed out above, one of the hardest things about managing behaviour is that you have to try to react in a way that is not natural for most of us. If somebody is difficult, rude or abusive towards you, the instinctive reaction is to fight back, whether this is by shouting, hitting out or running away. Unfortunately, these responses do not help us deal with poor behaviour from our children, or encourage them to have better behaviour in the future.

Bear in mind that your children are learning from you at all times, and this is particularly so in your reactions when they do something wrong. You are the adult, and it is up to you not to lose your cool. Imagine how a child feels when she sees her parent lose self-control or get completely furious. She might either feel very upset, or alternatively it could encourage her to misbehave again to see a repeat performance from you.

There are a number of reasons why it is so important to stay calm:

■ It will help you to deal with the situation in the best possible way. If you are feeling angry or wound up, you will not be able to respond rationally. You might blow up minor things into something more major, when it's not really necessary. Alternatively, you might allow yourself to get dragged into a heated argument with your child when the best thing to do is to calm the situation down.

■ It shows a good example of appropriate behaviour to your children. You are modelling 'good' behaviour for them all the time. If they see you lose your rag they will think this is how they can behave as well.

■ It can help calm and quieten an over-excited or confrontational child. This is your job as a parent. Your child has not yet learnt how to control her responses when she gets angry. As an adult, you should be able to do this at least a little better than your child.

Here are some tips that will help you maintain that calm reaction, no matter how tough it gets:

■ *See it as the child's problem* Try not to see poor behaviour as being deliberately directed at you: it most likely isn't. Very few of us deliberately misbehave to hurt or upset someone else, especially at an early age. Children are not yet able to fully control their actions. In fact the same applies to many of us as adults as well. Remember that if your child has not yet learnt how to behave properly, it is your responsibility to help teach her, rather than to resent her for this.

■ *Accept that it's not easy* Think about how easily you get wound up, either by misbehaviour, or just when you're having a bad time. Now think about how much more difficult it must be for your child. Accept that behaving well is not easy for your child, and you will be less likely to get angry.

■ *Don't get defensive* When someone 'attacks' us by being rude, disobedient or confrontational, it is all too easy to become defensive. It might feel like your child is deliberately aiming the misbehaviour at you, but this is probably not the case. Try not to get defensive when faced with difficult behaviour. If you do become defensive you are likely to lose your cool, and this will not help you deal with the situation or with your child.

Caring

The fifth C stands for 'caring'

It's tempting to believe that in order to be caring we must allow our children to do exactly what they want. In fact, being caring often means the opposite. Parents who care want the best for their children, and this means showing them what good behaviour is. That way we can help them understand the 'rules' of our society, preparing them for when they go out into the big wide world, and have to manage their behaviour on their own. Being firm doesn't mean that you don't care.

There are lots of different ways that you can take a more caring approach as a parent. Here are a few ideas for you to consider:

- *Make the most of them* Our children are only young for a very short time. Once their childhood has gone, we cannot get it back. Sometimes we lose sight of this fact, and get into a frame of mind where we see them as a cause of friction rather than a source of love and enjoyment. Do make the most of the good times together. Enjoy a cuddle with your child if she is upset; take the trouble to listen when she is unhappy. Find as many ways as you can to show how much you care, rather than keeping your love inside.

- *Give your time* Our time and attention are two of the most valuable things we can give to our children. I know how hard it is to spare time when you're busy either at work or around the home. This is especially so for parents of a number of children. But if you give your time as much as possible, and show how much you care, this will inevitably help the relationship between you and your family.

41

■ *Take their thoughts and feelings seriously* It is sometimes tempting to brush off our children's feelings, to imagine that they are just being 'silly' when they get upset. Do try to take your children's concerns seriously, for instance taking the time to chat through things when your child is scared. This will help you show how much you care. It will help your child understand that you are only being firm with her because you love her and want the best for her.

■ *Remember what it was like to be a child* Try to put yourself in your child's shoes sometimes, to understand what she is thinking and how she is feeling. When I think back to my childhood, things seemed to matter much more than they do now. Events or comments that might appear unimportant to me as an adult, often meant the world to me as a child. If you can put the clock back on occasions, and place yourself inside your child's head, you might be able to understand better why she behaves as she does.

■ *Explain what you do* When you are forced to crack down on poor behaviour, take the time to explain why you have to do this. Show your child that you are not being firm for your own sake, but for her benefit instead. Again, this is all part of showing that you are a caring parent. The idea is to develop a partnership in which you work together with your children to get things right.

■ *Explain the sanctions you give* On a similar note, when you do have to give a punishment, it pays to explain exactly what is going on. You might talk about why this particular sanction has been earned, how it could be avoided in the future, and so on.

■ *Always look for the positive* At all times, it really is worth looking for the positive when it comes to dealing with our children. Catch your child being good, and praise her to the skies. This will help you show the caring, loving side of yourself as a parent. Managing behaviour is not just about dealing with the difficult times, it's also about encouraging and helping your child to get it right.

Careful

The sixth C stands for 'careful'

When we're dealing with children it can be tempting to brush off their thoughts and feelings in the belief that, as adults, we know best. Because they are smaller than us, we might sometimes treat our children in a way that suggests they are less important than us, often without realizing that this is what we're doing.

As I pointed out above, when we are young things seem to matter so much more: we are so much more vulnerable to insecurity. What you might see as you snapping because you're in a bad mood, could in fact feel really hurtful to your child. Children do find it hard to be rational in the same way as we are as adults, and this applies particularly to an understanding of other people's emotions. For example, if you get angry with your child she might imagine that this means you don't love her anymore, whereas in fact you're simply feeling stressed.

Here are some tips that will help you treat your own children with the care and consideration that we all deserve:

■ *Treat them as you would any adult* If you were working in an office, you would never dream of telling a fellow worker to 'shut up', saying to them 'don't be stupid', or shouting at them out of turn. Unfortunately it is all too easy for these approaches to happen when we're dealing with our own children. It might be that you're feeling particularly tired or stressed, or perhaps your child is being especially difficult. Do try as often as you can to treat your children as you would any other adult, no matter how much they test you.

■ *Put yourself in their shoes* Any comment that you make to your child will be as powerful (if not more so) than if you made it to another adult. Try to step into your children's shoes and understand how what you say or do might look from their point of view. Being able to see and understand another person's perspective on a situation is a vital part of good behaviour management.

■ *Avoid sarcasm at all costs* As a teacher (and as a parent), I

43

must admit to resorting to sarcasm on a number of occasions. However, I'm always aware afterwards that it was not actually the right thing to do. As adults, we understand what sarcasm means, and we might even find it funny (although probably not when someone is sarcastic to us). Children are not yet able to understand this form of wit, and instead they may take it to heart. Try to think before you speak, to help you avoid that cutting, sarcastic comment that might do damage to your relationship with your child.

- *Try not to laugh at them* I know how easy it is to laugh at a child, especially when they get upset over something that seems unimportant, or when they do something silly. Unfortunately, children can take it the wrong way if an adult laughs at them. Do try to take your children's feelings seriously, aiming not to laugh if at all possible, unless you are sharing a joke.

Creative

The seventh and final C stands for 'creative'

Finally, there is plenty of room for creativity when it comes to being a parent. Creativity can mean many different things. It might be experimenting with new rewards, to see whether they are effective. It could be about finding interesting or original ways to encourage your child to behave better.

Children usually have a very strong sense of creativity. They love to use their imaginations, for instance going along with stories or fictions that you build for them. They also love to get involved with creative projects, for example helping you to create a chart on which positive behaviour can be rewarded.

Below you will find some ideas about how you can become a more creative parent to your child. I give ideas about managing behaviour and also suggestions for using creativity to help your child's development, and to improve the relationship you have together. Once you get started in using these creative approaches, you will probably find yourself thinking up loads of new ones of your own. Let your own imagination run riot when you're trying to find some more of these creative ideas to use in your own home.

Creativity and managing behaviour

■ *Experiment with new ideas and approaches* Don't be afraid to try out new ideas when it comes to managing your children's behaviour. The fear that an idea might fail often keeps us from trying out some experimental approaches that could actually work really well. In fact, in order to succeed, we need to up our failure rate and take risks on occasions. For instance, you might try a fun and original sanction, such as asking your child to stand on one leg and sing 'Humpty Dumpty' at the top of her voice. The fun element in such unusual ideas will help you build a better relationship with your child.

■ *Use the world of the imagination* Children do love the whole idea of stories and make-believe. They are brilliant at jumping into fictional worlds in a wholehearted way, an ability that we seem to lose as we become adults. We might create these imaginative worlds for our children, or let them come up with ideas of their own. You can use some of these imaginative ideas to help you control your child's behaviour. For instance, if I want my students to move around the classroom very quietly, I tell them to imagine that they are walking over a sleeping monster's back, and they must not wake him. This gives them the inspiration to behave in exactly the way that I want! Make behaving well fun for your children, and it will take very little effort to get them to comply.

■ *Look for different ways of solving problems* When you are faced with a problem, try to think laterally to come up with a new and creative solution. Aim to focus on positive approaches and rewards, rather than instantly turning to the negative use of sanctions. For instance, if your child refuses to sit properly in her chair for dinner, you could work with her to dress it up as a throne. Then when you want her to sit down for meals, you could put a toy crown on her head, and call her the 'queen of the chair'. This positive, original approach takes the focus away from the negative 'you must sit in your chair or else'

45

approach, and instead places it firmly on a more positive, reward-based idea of making the chair irresistible. You may well find that this solves the problem without any need for handing out sanctions.

■ *Find creative ideas for sanctions and rewards* Similarly, why not try to come up with some creative ideas for sanctions and rewards. For example, with a child who is keen on football, you could relate your sanctions to the sport, by making yellow and red cards like a referee uses during matches. When you have to sanction her, you could hand her a yellow card, with a warning that she will be 'sent off' with a red card if she earns a second one.

■ *Using fictional approaches* All children love stories, and they are quick to dive wholeheartedly into a fictional world. We can help encourage this aspect of our children's personalities by using fictional ideas with them. We can also use these fictional approaches to help encourage good behaviour, and discourage poor behaviour. For instance, you could use a hand puppet or a cuddly toy to respond to your child's behaviour 'in role', using it to distract her if she is misbehaving, or to comfort her if she is upset. The puppet might speak in a funny or sad voice to get your child's attention.

■ *The power of distraction* Distraction can be a very helpful strategy when you need to divert your child away from inappropriate behaviour. Be creative in the ideas you use to distract your child. For instance, you might make funny noises, blow on her tummy to tickle her, pretend to be a monkey, and so on. Again, the key to being creative is to unleash the big kid that lurks inside us all!

Creativity, development and better relationships

■ *Be a 'big kid' yourself* The key to creative parenting is for you not to be afraid to be a big kid yourself on occasions. This means not being afraid to muck in, to be a bit silly or stupid when you're dealing with your child. As we get older, we do tend to put the childlike side of ourselves behind us. This is a real shame, and when you have children of your own, you get the chance to revisit your own younger, freer days. The more childlike you can be with your child, the stronger the connection you should make with her creative and imaginative side.

■ *Developing imaginative play* There are so many great toys available these days, that it is easy to find something to capture your child's imagination. However, I do wonder whether these toys mean that we forget how powerful our children's imaginations can be. Try giving your children some objects that will push them to develop their imagination, and then work alongside them to see what you might create together. These imaginative play activities are great for getting several children working together, bouncing ideas off each other and developing better relationships between siblings. For example:

- ■ An empty cardboard box might become a huge post box into which they can post letters, or it could become a boat that they can 'sail' around the world.

- ■ An old sheet could become a magic carpet, on which your children read stories to each other, or a tent under which they shine torches.

■ *Let's get messy!* Sometimes it can be great fun, and a really good experience, to get messy with your children. I know how tempting it is to avoid these activities, because the last thing we want is a house that looks like a disaster area, and yet more tidying up to do! There is less and less time in school these days for these type of activities, so doing them at home with your children will help ensure that they get a rounded education. Spend some time getting messy with your child, and this will help bring out the big kid in you both. Why not try:

- ■ Some water play, for instance filling up a bowl with water and trying out different objects to see whether they sink or float.

- ■ Getting the paints out and having some fun with doing hand and footprints.

- ■ In the summer, getting out into the garden where there are loads of opportunities for messy play (and where you won't need to tidy up!), including sand pits, digging and so on.

FOUR

Behaviour Through the Ages

The way that our children behave changes over time. From the baby who understands very little about what 'behaviour' means, to the toddler who knows what he wants, and isn't afraid to let you know it, to the modern 'tweenager' who is on the cusp of puberty. In this chapter I look at behaviour through the different ages in the first ten years, from the baby right up to the pre-teen.

In fact, when it comes to managing behaviour there are many strategies that will work as well with a baby and in the teenage years and beyond, with only small changes. At the end of this chapter I give a very brief introduction to some strategies for dealing with the teenager – a time when your child is on the road to becoming an adult, and very often the techniques you use will have to be adapted to suit the new situation you face together.

The advice that I give throughout this book is very wide ranging, and will help you deal with the behaviour of children of all different ages. There are some ideas and tips, though, that will work best at particular points in a child's life. In this chapter I give an outline of how your child might behave at each stage. I also give advice that applies specifically to these times in your child's life.

As your child grows up, he will become more and more aware of what good and bad behaviour means. He will also become increasingly able to control his own responses. By the time he starts at school, hopefully he should be able to take responsibility for his own actions, and understand the potential consequences of what he does. If you can achieve this as a parent, I guarantee you that there will be many teachers out there who will thank you for it!

Being a baby

Being a tiny baby must be a bit like landing on an alien planet. You don't understand what anything is and you don't speak a single word of the language. Even though you work hard to communicate your thoughts and feelings, you find it almost impossible to make people understand what you're trying to put across to them.

The first way that babies try to tell us what they want is by crying or screaming. This is one of the few methods they have to communicate to us what is going on in their minds and in their bodies. One scream will tell you that your baby is hungry, another will tell you that he is tired, yet another will show you that he is bored. Your baby will also be communicating his inner state through the signals that he gives with his body, for instance tugging at his ear or yawning when he is tired.

When your baby cries, it's hard for you to hear and understand the different noises that he makes. In fact, it has been shown that a baby's cries are differentiated very early on, as he tries to communicate his varying needs to you. It is also difficult for us to 'read' a baby's body language, particularly when he is our first child. It must be very frustrating for him that we stupid adults just don't seem to understand what he is 'saying'!

At this stage of life, a child has little or no idea about the world in which he or she lives. During the first few weeks, the tiny baby doesn't even know who his parents are. His actions are entirely instinctive: he is simply responding to his immediate needs for sleep, food and comfort. In return, we as his parents respond in a similarly instinctive way when he asks for our help.

It is a very natural process to deal quickly with the wishes of a tiny crying baby, and it is at all times exactly the right thing to do. You might have seen those heartbreaking pictures of orphanages in eastern bloc countries, where the babies were left alone, trapped in their beds, crying for attention. If no one comes to a baby when he cries, he learns that it is not worth the bother. In his mind, he is already making a link that tells him: there's no point in expressing what I want, because no one comes to give it to me. This is very damaging to a child's development, particularly at this earliest stage. Our babies need to feel loved and cared for. During the early weeks and months your job as a parent is to give him these feelings as much as you are humanly able to do.

Baby behaviour

When they first come into the world, babies are to a certain extent a 'blank slate', especially when it comes to behaviour. It is now generally accepted that elements of both nature (our genetic make-up) and nurture (our upbringing) play a part in how we turn out as people. Although we cannot influence our baby's pre-existing personality, we can certainly have a strong impact on his experiences of his world.

A baby's brain develops in two ways: firstly by the natural maturing of the brain as an organ of the body, and secondly by his interactions with his environment. Right from the word 'go', his brain is making those vital connections that will help him become a thinking and intelligent being. It is up to us as parents to help him make the right connections, and this includes learning how he should behave.

When they are tiny, babies have absolutely no idea of the rules and requirements of the society in which they live. This is why they have no concept about what good or bad behaviour actually is. Babies cannot 'behave themselves' because they do not understand anything beyond their immediate selves.

Surprisingly quickly, even the smallest babies begin to make connections and start to understand their world. They don't know what we're saying, although they very quickly pick up the meaning of the word 'no'. (Perhaps this should tell us something about how negative we tend to be with our children!) Even though they don't yet understand what words mean, babies are able to pick up a lot of signals in other ways. They might hear a particular tone in your voice, or notice the way that you are using your face or body. You can find a lot more information about parent/child communication in Chapter 6, which deals with the huge variety of ways in which we can send signals to our children.

The very young child learns about his world mainly through interacting with it. He has no idea about what is dangerous and what isn't, and he doesn't understand why we want him to do certain things, and not to do others. He must try to work all this out for himself. He will do this mostly through experimentation, for instance by seeing what happens if he behaves in certain ways.

Managing your baby's behaviour

Although babies have very little understanding about behaviour, this does not mean that we cannot start working on the basics with them. This early teaching will mainly take the form of starting to make it clear what we do and do not want. You might feel that you should allow your baby as much freedom as possible, but there will clearly be situations where this is not the right thing to do. For instance you might say 'no' very firmly when your baby tries to chew on a cable, removing him immediately from the danger. He will not understand what you are doing, or why you are doing it, but you will be starting to send him signals about his behaviour by taking this approach.

We also teach our babies by the example we set, particularly about how people should treat each other. For example, you will be caring for your baby, cuddling him, feeding him and trying to comfort him when he gets upset. He will begin to learn how love is shown, and consequently how he too can show his love for you. So it is by about one year old, your baby might be willing to give you a well-deserved kiss for all your hard work so far!

Your baby's ability to learn by example means that he will be picking up on the negative behaviours that he sees from you, as well as these more positive things. From the very first days, you should take care about the way that you behave around your child. For instance, if he hears you repeatedly losing your temper and swearing at your partner, he will be mentally filing this behaviour away for future reference. If you can learn to improve your own behaviour right from the start, this will help 'train' you for when your child is old enough to repeat what you say and do!

Here are a few tips about how you can start to manage your baby's behaviour from the very earliest days. I've split this advice up into 'What to do' and 'What not to do', to show you both the right and wrong approaches.

What to do

- *Start making connections* The very first thing you can do for your baby is to start making connections between his behaviour and its consequences. You can do this by applying the certainty, clarity and consistency that I've already discussed. Give your baby the message that every time he does a particular behaviour, this is how mummy/daddy will react. Your reaction should take into account that your child is only a baby. For instance, although giving sanctions will be pretty pointless at this stage, you will start to remove him from a situation where he is putting himself in danger. This will help to build his concepts of right and wrong: of what is and is not allowed.

- *Start setting the boundaries* In the first year of your child's life, you can start to work out what you do and do not want when it comes to behaviour. This is actually not as easy as it might sound, because often what might later be seen as misbehaviour is at this stage very educational for your baby. For instance, do you mind if your baby tears up your newspaper, or if he pulls all the clothes out of the drawers in his room? If you let these behaviours go now, it will be harder to clamp down on them in the future. By establishing the boundaries for your baby right from the word go, and sticking to these ideas consistently, you will set yourself up for an easier ride as your child gets older.

- *Start to create routines* Routines give your baby a feeling of security, a way of understanding what is coming next. These patterns help your baby to know what is expected

52

of him in each situation, for instance the idea that being put in his cot means that he is about to go to sleep, or that bath, book and milk means it is bedtime. I look in lots of detail at the idea of creating structures and routines in Chapter 5 (pp. 79–85).

- *Don't forget to focus on the positive* When you're looking at your baby's behaviour, do remember to catch him being good as often as possible. When he does do something well, make a big deal out of it, particularly by using lots of praise. You might say 'good boy' or 'clever boy', using an enthusiastic tone of voice. He will soon pick up on which behaviours earn him your attention. Make sure these are the positive rather than the negative ones, and he will be keen to repeat the good behaviour. For example, as you dress your baby you might say 'good boy' as you put the vest over his head and as you pull each arm through. Over time, he will learn to do this for himself, as a way to gain your praise.

- *Focus on sounds* It's important to remember that tiny babies cannot yet see the world around them very clearly. The most strongly developed senses at this stage are smell and sound. Let your baby know when something is 'wrong' by using sound, for instance a firm tone of voice. This does not mean shouting, simply sounding very definite and certain.

- *Use facial expressions* Although your baby cannot see a lot of the world around him, his parents' faces are of huge importance to him. Make your face express your feelings, again focusing on the positive rather than the negative ones. Get up close to your baby and show him when you are delighted with him, for instance by widening your eyes and giving him a great big fat smile!

- *Don't expect instant results* Please don't get too worried if these ideas don't seem to work instantly. Bear in mind that a lot of repetition will be required before any of this will even begin to sink into your baby's brain. Stick with it, though, and this early training will stand you in very good stead when your darling little baby becomes an awkward toddler, and things start to get more difficult!

- *Keep it simple* At this stage, you are looking for the big yes/ no ideas. Focus on what's really important when it comes to your baby's behaviour. To my mind, this should include teaching your baby about what is dangerous to him, and also about how to behave well towards other people. For example, if your baby scratches at your face or bites you, you might put him away from you very firmly, saying 'no' and making it clear by your facial expression and tone of voice that this behaviour is not going to be allowed.

■ *Use distraction* Distractions works well for children of all different ages. As a behaviour management technique it is particularly useful for the very small baby. He might get involved in misbehaving, and be unable to break himself away from the situation. There is little point at this stage in debating the issue, or in trying to 'sanction' him. By using a quick distraction, such as shaking a noisy toy, you can often stop poor behaviour in its tracks.

■ *Use removal* Another excellent way to deal with a baby who is misbehaving is simply to remove him from the situation. This applies particularly to the baby who is doing something dangerous. As well as removing your child from dangerous situations, it is also a very good idea to remove temptation from your child's reach. Although a certain amount of exploration is necessary for our children to learn, you will save yourself a great deal of stress if you put really dangerous or potentially 'naughty-making' items out of your baby's way, at least for a little while. Once he is older, and more able to understand, you can gradually reintroduce these things. (Of course it is vital to keep potentially life-threatening items such as medicines and household cleaners permanently locked away from children of any age.)

■ *Bear in mind the power of personality* I know from meeting lots of different babies, that individual personality is a powerful factor in how your child will behave throughout his life. If you find that your baby seems to be particularly 'difficult', bear in mind that this is not necessarily as a result of anything that you might have done as a parent. It could be that you simply have a very demanding baby, who might or might not turn out to be an equally demanding child. If this is the case, you will need to stick even more carefully to the strategies outlined in this book, to help him learn how to behave.

- *Above all else, demonstrate your love* Above everything else that we need to do with our babies, showing them love is the most important thing of all. A baby who feels secure, loved and wanted will grow up to be a well-adjusted, loving and hopefully well-behaved child.

What not to do

- *Don't give up* You'll need to stick at the ideas given above, and throughout this book, allowing plenty of time for your baby to get the message. Although it may take many months before you see any progress, you are in fact setting yourself up for an easier time by establishing the ground rules right from the start.

- *Shouting won't work* There is absolutely no point at all in shouting at a baby. All it will achieve is an upset baby, and a very frazzled parent. Learn how to control your emotions now – you'll need plenty of practice! Learning how not to lose your temper is very hard to do, especially when your child is really testing the limits later on in his life.

- *Don't be too hard on yourself* Although we all know that shouting at a baby (and indeed a child) is not really the best approach, of course we all make this mistake from time to time. Please don't beat yourself up if and when you do. I fully understand what it's like being a parent, especially during those difficult first few months. Sleep deprivation is probably the biggest culprit when it comes to us losing our tempers. It's almost like a form of torture when you haven't had a decent night's sleep in months. Don't be too hard on yourself when you make mistakes – both you and your baby are learning how to get along together, and this will inevitably take some time.

- *Don't be too hard on your baby* As you try to establish some ground rules for behaviour, please don't be too hard on your baby when he gets it wrong. Remember that in this first year of his life, he is learning huge amounts every single day. He has to learn how to move, how to talk, how to play, how to understand what people are saying to him. It really is a tough life being a baby!

Toddlers and the 'terrible twos'

We've all heard the horror stories about the 'terrible twos'. The image of your child throwing himself flat in the supermarket, banging his fists on the floor, and screaming at the top of his voice, is enough to scare even the bravest of parents. In fact, though, this difficult stage is absolutely vital to your child's development, and it should be welcomed rather than feared.

The 'terrible twos' does not need to be so 'terrible' after all. It should indeed be possible to enjoy the experience of watching your child grow as he moves through this important time in his life. The key thing is to stick at the ideas that I give in this book. If you can achieve this, you will be able to move your child quickly through this stage of his development, and get on with the process of enjoying your relationship.

The phase that we call the 'terrible twos' can actually start from as early as around one year old. The tantrums and difficult behaviour that you will most probably experience do happen for some very good reasons. If you can understand what's going on behind all this difficult behaviour, it will help you to deal with the challenges that you're likely to face. Here are some thoughts about why your child will test your patience so much during this stage of his life.

- *Breaking away mentally* The key to the 'terrible twos' lies in the fact that your child is starting to break away from you, his parents. He is beginning to understand that he is a separate person with his own thoughts, feelings and wishes. Once he understands that he can make it clear what he wants, and sometimes even get his own way by doing so, he moves into this phase that we all seem to dread so much.

- *Breaking away physically* It's no coincidence that many of these developmental changes seem to come hand in hand with the physical ones. As soon as a baby learns to walk (or even to crawl), he becomes instantly more independent from his parents, simply because he can physically move himself away from you. Similarly, as soon as a child can talk, he can start to express what he wants, and to assert his own wishes.

■ *Developing a sense of self* Babies have no sense of themselves as being separate people. They are very closely attached to their parents, and for the first year or so they see themselves pretty much as an extension of you. Once they begin to develop this sense of self, it leads them to an understanding that they can behave specifically in the way that they want. His sense of what he does and doesn't like, and what he does and doesn't want to do, is all part of your child developing his own personality.

■ *The ability to say 'no'* As he grows up, your child learns that he can say 'no' if he doesn't want to do something. Indeed, sometimes when he says 'no' we agree to his wishes, and allow him not to do what he doesn't want to. For instance if he decides that he doesn't like the taste of particular foods, then we might allow him not to eat these things. On the other hand, he must also learn that sometimes he will have to do things that he doesn't necessarily enjoy. It's a lesson of life that we must all learn, but it's not always an easy one to take on board, and it can lead to lots of misbehaviour along the way as the boundaries are tested.

■ *Learning the 'rules'* At this stage in his life, your child is still learning about what is and isn't allowed in the society within which he lives. This is what you, as his parents, must teach him. You will help to show him what he can and can't do by demonstrating to him what the consequences of certain behaviours will be. Remember that this applies to positive behaviours as well as to negative ones. It is then up to him to decide how he wishes to behave, and whether he is willing to accept the consequences when he does do something wrong.

■ *Testing the boundaries* At this stage in their lives, our children are seeing what will happen when they push at the limits. It is as though a switch goes on in the child's head, and he suddenly realizes that he doesn't actually have to do what you tell him. By testing the boundaries your child learns more about what you will and won't allow him to do. This is why it is so important to keep your boundaries very clear and firm, and to be confident that eventually you will get what you want.

■ *Understanding his own power* Similarly, your child is

57

beginning to understand the power that he has over his parents. For instance, he starts to realize that if you are in a public place such as a supermarket, his ability to embarrass you offers him a powerful weapon in getting what he wants. Experimenting with the use of this power is, again, all part of the process of growing up.

■ *Trying to get what 'I want'* With a little baby, we try as hard as we can to meet his every need. Once our children get a little older, though, they have to learn that 'I want' doesn't always mean 'I get'. For instance, a child who is a little bit peckish does not need to be fed instantly. Instead, he must learn that it is okay for him to be a little bit hungry and that sometimes he might have to wait for his dinner.

■ *Attention-seeking* You will probably find that a fair amount of the poor behaviour that you experience from your child at this stage is actually an attempt to get your attention. This attention, as I have already mentioned, is one of the things that our children most want from us. As our children develop, they quickly come to understand how best to gain their parents' attention. Misbehaving, especially in public, is one excellent way to do just this! Try not to see this attention-seeking behaviour as a deliberate attempt to embarrass you, though. Young children are not that calculating. What your toddler is starting to do is to make a connection between what he does, and your response. If your first reaction to misbehaviour is to lavish your attention on your child (even if that attention is shouting at him), then don't be surprised if he starts to misbehave more regularly.

■ *Mood* Our mood has an amazing impact on the way that we behave. Consider how your own mood affects your behaviour, for instance the way that you might 'niggle' at your partner when you're feeling tired or run down. The same factors also affect your child, particularly at this stage when he does not yet understand how to cope for himself. If your child is tired, hungry, upset or bored, you will probably experience an increase in that 'terrible two' behaviour.

■ *You're learning too* It's my belief that the 'terrible twos' are not just about our children learning to assert themselves.

This stage is also about us as parents, learning how to make the transition between looking after a baby, and dealing with a young child. When our children are tiny babies, we work as hard as we possibly can to meet their every need. This is particularly so because we cannot fully understand what they want from us. The moment your baby cries, you probably rush to attend to him, particularly if he is your first child. The urge to stop him crying is very strong, an instinctive reaction that it is almost impossible to ignore. Eventually, though, we start to realize that sometimes our children can't always have exactly what they want the moment that they want it. For instance, sometimes a child will whinge or cry just because he is bored. Well, we all have to be bored sometimes, and we learn to put up with it, or to entertain ourselves. As parents we have to start to make this mental leap once our children reach the toddler stage.

Dealing with the 'terrible twos'

There are various strategies that you can use to help you survive this phase of your children's life. As I point out throughout this book, none of these ideas is hard to put into place, it's sticking with them that is really difficult. Here are some tips that will help you live through the 'terrible twos', hopefully without too much stress.

■ *Keep your expectations clear* At this stage the most important thing you can do for your child is to keep your expectations crystal clear. You will be under lots of pressure to 'give in', especially when your child is throwing the most monumental of all tantrums. You must stick at it, though. You will not be doing your toddler any favours if you start to falter at this stage. Remember to share your expectations with your child as well, by letting him know what it is that you actually want from him.

■ *Be confident* If you are confident about what you want from your child, this confidence will communicate itself to him, for instance through the way that you talk and also through the body language and other signals that you use. That is not to say that he will necessarily do as you ask, though. Again, stick at it and eventually this phase of pushing at the limits will pass.

■ *Don't give your attention for the wrong reasons* For the young child, misbehaving is often a sure-fire way to grab his parents' attention. This is particularly so for the child who is throwing a no holds barred, over the top, full steam ahead, tantrum. It's incredibly hard to stop yourself, but do try not to give the reward of your attention for poor behaviour. If you do, you will start to create a connection in his mind between misbehaving and gaining your attention. Bear in mind that although shouting at your child is a punishment of sorts, it is still a form of attention. If you're brave enough, and the situation allows, you might try completely ignoring him and just letting him get on with it (keeping an eye on him to ensure that he doesn't hurt himself). Alternatively, you could try removing him from the immediate area to a safe place where he can calm himself down.

■ *Give your attention for the right reasons* On the other hand, when your child is being good, for instance playing quietly with his toys, it is all too easy to simply overlook him. The key to overcoming attention-seeking misbehaviour is to learn to make a big deal of it when your child is doing the right thing. I know how tempting it is to ignore a well-behaved child, in the belief that if you leave him alone he'll continue to behave well. What you want, though, is to make a very clear connection between appropriate behaviours and gaining your attention. Make a big deal out of it every time you see your child doing something right. Go over the top, making it clear that you are very pleased by your face, your tone of voice, the use of rewards and so on. That way, he will be more likely to repeat the behaviour that you do want, rather than the behaviour that you don't.

■ *Introduce rewards and sanctions* As soon as your child is able to understand, start to introduce the idea that some behaviours will be rewarded, while others will be punished. Making the connection between behaviour and its consequences is vital in getting your child to behave as you wish. Chapter 7 deals in lots of detail with how to use rewards and sanctions.

- *Make it fun to say 'yes'* It can be incredibly frustrating to have to deal with a child who has just learnt to say 'no', and who is flexing his refusal muscles. Do bear in mind that learning to make his wishes clear is all part of developing his own personality. This will of course include his personal likes and dislikes. Unfortunately, not all of these will be acceptable to you as his parent, for instance, the child who point-blank refuses to have a bath for days on end. Rather than trying to force your child to do something that he simply doesn't want to do, try instead to make it fun to say 'yes'. For example you could get in the bath yourself, filling it with bubble bath and toys, and letting your child watch you splashing around and having fun.

- *Start to make him 'put up'* As our baby moves into the toddler stage of development, you are entitled to start making him 'put up' with certain things. The 'spoilt' child, who always gets what he wants, will put the maximum pressure on you as a parent. He will also not fare well when he has to behave himself in situations outside the home, such as when he starts school. Begin to teach your child that sometimes he will just have to 'put up and shut up' (although aim to phrase this more politely). You can do this quite simply by ignoring him if he whinges or by offering a positive alternative, or a distraction.

- *Try not to worry* If you're out and about with your child, and he throws a major tantrum, it can be extremely embarrassing. Do try not to worry about what other people think, because this might make you give in on your clear and certain expectations about his behaviour. Don't let him have power over you in this way. The sooner you establish the boundaries for him, the better and easier both your lives will be. If you do give in because of the embarrassment factor, you will simply delay the day when the tantrums diminish and eventually disappear.

Behaviour: the early years

I define the 'early years' at the stage in your child's life when he has moved beyond his baby days, and hopefully through the 'terrible twos' and out the other side. The years between three and five years old can and should be a very pleasurable experience for both of you (as, indeed, should all the time you spend with your child).

If you have gone back to work, your child might be at nursery or with a child minder during the day. Even if he is at home with you, it will not be long before he is ready to start at nursery school. At this stage your child is beginning to master the basic skills, widening his vocabulary and developing his ability with language.

At around the age of three, your child will start to be able to play with other children, and this can lead to some problems of its own. At first, playing together with friends is often more a case of playing alongside them. It takes time for genuine collaborative play to develop. Your child needs to understand that other people have feelings too, and this is a difficult concept for him to grasp.

Here are some of my top tips for dealing with behaviour in the early years.

- *Stick with it* At this stage you should aim to stick to all the ideas that I've outlined in this book. You might not be seeing the immediate results that you'd hoped for, but bear in mind that your child is still in the process of learning how to behave. The more often you can repeat the same approaches, the better and quicker your child will make those vital connections between what he does and its consequences.

- *Don't worry about setbacks* Sometimes you will experience setbacks with your child's behaviour. You might be feeling confident that the tantrums are over and done with, when out of the blue another one happens. The occasional setback is inevitable, as your child continues to test the boundaries to see what is and isn't allowed. Try not to worry too much when this does happen – it doesn't mean that all your hard work is not paying off.

- *Start to use delayed gratification* I explain this term in detail in Chapter 7 (p. 120). It basically means that, instead of always using immediate rewards (or sanctions), you should now start to develop the idea that your child might have to behave well several times to earn a bigger reward. For instance, you might offer a treat such as a trip to the zoo, for continued good behaviour over a period of days or weeks.

■ *Prepare him for school* As your child begins at nursery, or as he moves up into the Reception class, you can start to help him to develop and maintain the appropriate behaviour in school. Following the advice in this book will have helped you lay the ground rules, and many of the ideas that I have discussed here will be continued and built upon by his teacher at school. If he does get into trouble for poor behaviour, then talk this through with him. You may find that your child accuses his teacher of being unfair, or of picking on him. When you sit down to discuss the situation, though, you will probably find that there was a very good reason for any sanctions that the teacher had to give. Try to support your child's teacher as a figure of authority, rather than taking your child's side all the time. You can find lots more ideas about how to support your child at school in Chapter 9.

Behaviour: the middle years

I class the 'middle years' as covering the ages from about five to eleven years old. This is the time when your children start Year One, through to what is normally the end of the middle school, at Year Six. These can be some of the very best times in your relationship with your children. They are not yet old enough to have fully pulled away from their parents. This is a time before they have moved out into the big wide world, perhaps becoming cynical and losing some of that lovely innocence of the young child.

At this stage your child is still learning about the world in which he lives. He will be developing and even beginning to master most of the basic skills, such as speaking, reading and writing. He is learning how to communicate his thoughts and feelings, how to make friends and how to play coopera-tively. He is also becoming much more independent in taking care of himself, and is developing an understanding of other people's emotional states.

This is a time when your child is still full of energy and enthusiasm, so enjoy it while it lasts. Before you know it, he will be a teenager, with the attitude and hormones that make the secondary school years such a trial for some parents. You can find some tips and thoughts below about dealing with your child's behaviour during this stage.

- *Stick to the principles* As your child starts to behave well with less input from you as an adult, it is tempting to feel that you can let the boundaries relax a little. Although there is no harm in adapting the limits to suit the age of your child, do make sure that you stick to the principles that I've outlined in this book. For instance, know what your expectations are and keep them consistent.

- *Acknowledge that he's growing up* As your child gets older, you can use the fact that he's 'growing up' as a useful carrot for better behaviour. Make a point about his age, and the grown-up way that he should now be able to behave. For example, you might say something like 'Now that you're so much older, daddy knows how good you are at getting yourself ready for bed. Let's see you put your pyjamas on like a big boy.' This acknowledgement of increasing maturity is particularly useful for 'tweenagers' – those children on the verge of becoming teenagers. At this stage, we might allow a child to stay up slightly later, pointing out that this is possible because they are so much more mature and sensible, and asking them to still take responsibility for getting up on time in the morning.

- *But don't forget he's still young* The thought that your child is getting older might mean you begin not to see him as a young child anymore. Although he will be gaining more independence and maturity, don't forget that sometimes he will still need to be treated as your 'baby'. He might want comforting when he gets upset, a cuddle when he's had a bad day at school, and so on.

- *Make sure you continue to give attention for the right reasons* Similarly, you might find yourself needing to give your child less attention, because he is so much more able to do things for himself. He could be happily entertaining himself by playing extended games with his toys, and you might feel tempted to just let him get on with it. Don't forget to give positive reinforcement when he's doing the right thing, though, to emphasize and repeat the message that this is the behaviour that you do want. Similarly, don't be tempted to start giving him attention when he messes around.

- *Make him a 'helper'* At this stage, your child will be able to help you a great deal, both around the house and particularly with other children if you have them. Helping out adults is an excellent way of giving our children a chance to succeed, and of getting them to take on more grown-up attitudes and approaches. As a teacher, I often get my students to 'be teacher', writing up work on the board for me, or handing out materials. They love this grown-up role, particularly at this stage in their development. Make use of this fact with your own children, for instance asking an older child to help out in dressing or feeding his younger sibling.

- *Don't forget to play* As our children grow up, we might feel that they no longer need us to play with them, that they can quite happily entertain themselves. Do remember though that your attention is one of the most useful rewards of all. Taking time out to play with your children is not only an excellent way of encouraging continued good behaviour, but it is also fun for you both. Of course, I do know how difficult it can be to make time in our busy lives to play when we have so many other things to do, but it really is worth making the effort as often as you can. 'Playing' with your child can also include grown-up tasks, such as preparing a meal or doing the washing up together.

Teenage and 'tweenage' behaviour

Although this book is aimed at the parents of babies and young children, it is worth giving a quick rundown here about what happens to your child once they become a tween or teenager. After the relative peace of the years from five to about ten, the years between about eleven and sixteen are a time when all sorts of trouble can start up again. If you haven't set the boundaries early on, this can be a recipe for disaster when dealing with a difficult, hormonal teen.

This section looks briefly at why teenagers can cause their parents such problems, and also gives you some ideas to help you in dealing with behaviour issues at this age.

Why are teenagers so difficult?

■ *Making the break* As they move towards or into the teenage years, our children start to make the final break away from their parents, in preparation for becoming adults. As they make this break, you will probably find that they push at the boundaries and limits that you have set for them. This will particularly be so if you have set very strict and authoritarian guidelines for your child. You may need to adapt some of the less important boundaries at this stage.

■ *Influences at school* At this stage, outside influences become much stronger. Your teenager will be influenced by the behaviour and attitudes of the friends in his age group at school. Your young teenager might also begin to be influenced by the behaviour that he sees from older students. We are often influenced by what we see our elders doing, and the same applies to our children when they are at school. If the behaviour of the older students is good, and the culture of the school is one of good behaviour, then these influences can be very positive ones. On the other hand, if the school does not have an ethos of good behaviour, and he sees the older students misbehaving in more serious ways, he might pick up on this.

■ *'Street' influences* As well as being affected by what he sees from his classmates at school, your child might also pick up negative (or indeed positive) influences from his friends, from local 'gangs', or from the street culture that surrounds him.

■ *Making the transition* In addition to the above factors, the time in your child's life when he makes the change from primary to secondary school can also lead to some difficulties for 'tweenagers', in the time just before the teenage years begin. This transition comes at a time when children are undergoing lots of physical changes, and when the hormones are just starting to kick in. The change from primary to secondary is difficult for a number of reasons, and it's worth understanding what these are:

- They go from being the 'big' children at the top of the school, to being back in the lowest year group.
- They might be split up from the close friends that they have made in their primary school.
- They must deal with the change from having one teacher for most of their lessons, to having a different teacher for each subject.
- They have to move around between classrooms, rather than having one room where they are taught.
- This constant movement means that they must be very well organized, knowing what lesson is next, and having the correct equipment.
- The school itself will be bigger, and this can cause worries for the children. For instance, they are often scared of getting lost.
- Expectations of behaviour and work may be much tougher than at primary school.
- Sanctions, such as detentions, will probably be used more frequently.
- They will be receiving quite a lot of homework, from lots of different teachers, and this can be difficult to cope with.

What can I do about it?

- *Start to treat him as an adult* As your child grows into a young adult, you will need to start treating him as one. This might mean giving him more rights (and of course the responsibilities that go with these rights). You can find lots more information about rights and responsibilities in the RESPECT formula in Chapter 5.
- *Be open and honest* Try to be open and honest with your tween or teenager, for instance being willing to

acknowledge when you are finding his behaviour difficult, and the impact that it has on you as a person. By this stage, our children are able to empathize much more fully with other people, and this is an important part of their social and behavioural development. You might like to tell him more and more about how you are feeling – for instance letting him know if you are tired, stressed or upset. Encourage him to share his worries or problems with you, rather than keeping them to himself.

■ *Develop a sense of partnership* By the time they become teenagers, we will hopefully have been able to develop a strong sense of 'working together' with our children. This partnership will involve a two-way feeling of respect. If you want your teenager to respect you, then you must offer a similar amount of respect in return.

■ *Be flexible* As they grow older, our children start to question the demands we make of them, and will begin to expect a little more leeway. You will have to learn to be flexible as your child becomes a young adult, otherwise you are likely to experience more seriously confrontational attitudes.

■ *Let him learn from his mistakes* As your child becomes an older teenager, you can start to let him learn from his own mistakes. This will help him understand how to take responsibility for his own actions. For example, if he insists that he wants to stay up late on a school night, then why not let him? He will soon find out that getting up in the morning is hard after a late night.

■ *Adapt the rewards and sanctions you use* The type of rewards and sanctions you use will have to change at this stage. Although positive approaches and the use of praise will still be important, you may find that you have to turn as well to more materialistic types of 'carrot', such as money, CDs or trips.

■ *Support him during the transition at school* There are plenty of ways that you can help your pre-teen make the move from primary to secondary school. By supporting him during this transition, you will help avoid the 'blip' in behaviour and attitudes that sometimes occurs. You can find lots of advice about how to do this in Chapter 9 of this book.

FIVE

The RESPECT Formula

In this chapter I'm going to explain what I call the RESPECT formula. This formula is a series of ideas and approaches that can be used to build respect between you and your children. In my opinion, quality parenting is all about the giving and gaining of respect. It's a two-way street – we cannot ask our children to give us respect unless we earn it. Our aim should be to build a partnership in which we get what we request because our children respect us enough to give it. This respect will only be given if the requests we make are fair, and the way in which we enforce the boundaries seems reasonable.

We no longer live in a world where children must do what they're told without question; where they are seen and not heard, where adults are the ones in charge at all times. People are starting to see that children have a right to express their own opinions and feelings, that they cannot just be brushed off like in the so-called 'good old days'. Some people might think we've gone too far in the direction of being 'soft' on our children. Perhaps this has an element of truth, but in my opinion what we have now is certainly much better than what went before.

However, although I believe that children should be given a certain amount of personal freedom, this doesn't mean that it isn't still possible to have respect. What it does mean is that this respect must be earned – both by children from their parents, and vice versa. The RESPECT formula described in this chapter will help you to develop this two-way respect with your own children.

The ideas that I outline in this chapter are, once again, developed from my experience of working with many different children over the years. As a teacher, I have found myself able to give and gain two-way respect much of the time. The positive relationships that I have developed with my students are a wonderful example of how this two-way respect can work.

What does respect mean?

Everyone seems to use the word 'respect' these days, but how many of us actually think carefully about what it means? For me, a good summary of 'respect' would be 'treating others as you would want them to treat you'. This is why we need to set a good role model for our children if we want them to behave properly. I've listed below what I see as some of the key ideas behind the word 'respect' – what it does mean, and what it doesn't. You might have some more ideas of your own that you would add to this list.

Respect means being
- polite
- caring
- kind
- considerate
- thoughtful
- helpful

Respect means not

- being rude
- being unkind
- swearing
- mistreating property
- hurting others
- being aggressive

How, then, can we encourage this two-way respect between ourselves and our children? Below you'll find details of the RESPECT formula, which gives you a way of developing this respect within your own family. This formula stands for the following ideas:

> **R**ights and responsibilities
> **E**xpectations
> **S**tructures
> **P**ositivity
> **E**nergy
> **C**ommunication
> **T**raining

R'n'R: rights and responsibilities

The 'R' in the RESPECT formula stands for two key words: 'rights' and 'responsibilities'. These two ideas go together to make up a recipe for giving and getting respect.

A lot of people in our world don't even have the most basic rights. These basic rights include a right to clean water, to healthy food, to a roof over your head, the freedom to say what you want without fear of being persecuted and so on. We are very lucky that we can give our children rights beyond these most basic ones. It is up to us as parents to set these rights for our children. We need to decide how far we can or want to go in giving them rights beyond those that everyone deserves as a matter of course.

In return for giving our children these rights, they need to learn about the second R in the equation – responsibility. They must take responsibility for their own actions and behaviour, and this is where we as their parents come in. We have to help our children understand the idea that with rights come responsibilities. We have to teach them how to do this. Very young children do not understand this idea, so we have to help them to understand the concept. This understanding may take a while to come, so don't expect instant results with your own children.

It is very hard to find a balance between rights and responsibilities. We have to make some personal choices about how many rights and how much responsibility our children can cope with at any time in their lives. We also have to decide how much personal freedom they deserve or have earned. The balance that we choose will depend on a number of different factors, including:

- our style as parents (see Chapter 2)
- the age of our children
- how mature they are
- how 'streetwise' they are
- the safety of our local environment

R'n'R: some examples

Here are some examples to help you understand the idea of R'n'R. Notice how, with each right comes a responsibility.

Right To go to bed at the time you want (or at a later time than normal, as set by the parents).
Responsibility To get up on time for school, and in a fit state to work.

Right To go outside to play with your friends.
Responsibility To return home at a set time decided by the parents, or agreed with the child.

Right To own a pet.
Responsibility To help take care of the pet – feeding it, cleaning up after it, and so on.

Why should I use R'n'R?

Why, then, should we bother teaching our children about rights and responsibilities? Here are two of the key reasons for using this technique.

- *Developing a partnership* Using R'n'R will help you to develop a partnership with your children. The idea is that you work together to get along as best you possibly can. Aim to create mutual respect between you and your children. You are effectively saying that you respect your child enough to give her these rights. In return, she must respect you enough to take on the responsibilities.

- *Ownership of behaviour* Our ultimate aim as parents is to make our children responsible for their own behaviour. We must accept that we won't always be there to make the decisions for them, and that the sooner they can do this for themselves, the better it will be. We have to hand over some of the responsibility to our children sooner or later. If we do this, when they go to school, or later on in their lives, they will be able to make the right decisions about how to behave.

How do I use R'n'R?

There are various factors that you should take into account when introducing the idea of rights and responsibilities with your children. These will help you use R'n'R in the most effective way.

- *Introduce it gradually* Don't expect your child instantly to be able to take responsibility. Instead, it is much better gradually to introduce rights and the responsibilities that go along with them. This can be done in a drip-feed fashion so that the child gradually learns how these two ideas work together.

- *Make it clear what you're doing* Do talk about the whole idea of R'n'R with your child. Make it very clear that when you give her a right, she must also take on the responsibility that comes with it. If she cannot, or is unwilling to make the effort, then the right will be removed.

- *Judge the maturity of your child* How able your child is to cope with R'n'R will very much depend on the individual child. I'm afraid that I can't give you a list of rights and responsibilities, and tell you exactly the right age at which to introduce them. As parents, you alone can judge how mature your child is, and how ready she is to take on the R'n'R you might offer.

- *Judge your personal situation* The rights you offer will be dependent on the situation in which you find yourself. For instance, if the streets outside your home are very unsafe, you will not be able to let your child have the right to play outside on her own. Similarly, if your life is too busy or your home too small to accommodate a pet, then this right will not be available to your child.

What happens if my child won't take responsibility?

If you find that your child is not able to take responsibility, it may be that you have tried to introduce rights that she is not yet mature enough to cope with. If this is the case, try the following:

- *Take away the right* If your child refuses to take responsibility for her actions, then of course you can simply take away the right completely. By doing this, you show the child that she must take responsibility for her behaviour, or she will not be allowed the rights you have given her.

- *Lessen the right* Instead of taking away a right completely, you might choose instead to lessen it or add some kind of limits to it. For example, instead of having the right to go outside and play with friends for an extended period, you might instead set a time limit on outdoor play.

- *Make a gradual reintroduction* Once the rights have been removed or lessened, you can then gradually reintroduce them. The carrot or reward for taking responsibility is being given back the rights in full.

- *Use the right as a reward* Once we get beyond the most basic rights, everything else is really icing on the cake. This means that you can use the rights you give your child as a carrot or reward for good behaviour. If you see her taking responsibility for her actions, and doing it well, then you might give her a right as a reward. For instance, in return for helping with the washing up, you might give her the reward of watching an extra half hour of television.

Expectations

I read a wonderful quote once, in relation to the way that teachers view our students, and it goes something like this:

> If you see a child as what she is at the moment, then that's all she'll ever be. But if you view a child as someone really special, as having a huge amount of potential to be the best she can possibly be, then she may well live up to your expectations.

This quote sums up what expectations are all about – the setting of high goals and standards in the belief that every child can attain the very best. The idea is that you expect the absolute best from your children as a teacher. The same can apply to what you expect as a parent. You want your children to achieve all that they are capable of, and by setting the standards high you will help them to aim for the very top.

Below you'll find a five-step guide to the basic ideas behind using expectations with your child. This quick guide gives you an outline of the approach. You can find much more detail about how to work out and apply your expectations further on in this section.

Quick guide to expectations

1. Decide for yourself what your expectations are.
2. Make your expectations crystal-clear to your child.
3. Once you've decided on your expectations, stick to them like glue.
4. Expect your child to live up to your expectations. If she does, reward her.

5. If she doesn't live up to your expectations:
- ■ react with surprise, rather than anger
- ■ keep repeating your expectations over and over again
- ■ use sanctions if it is necessary
- ■ remember that eventually she will come to understand

Establishing your expectations

As you saw in the 'quick guide', the first step in using expectations is to establish exactly what it is you do actually want. This might sound very simple, but in fact it's actually quite hard to do.

Here's an exercise to help you develop your own ideas about 'good' behaviour, and to establish exactly what it is that you want from your child. This activity will help you to work out what your own expectations are.

'In a perfect world . . .'

Imagine that you live in a perfect world, where children behave in what you consider to be exactly the right way. Now write down up to 10 different points that sum up your 'perfect' situation. For example, one of your points might be 'My child is always polite.' Try to make your statements positive rather than negative ones, for instance saying 'My child uses appropriate language at all times', rather than 'My child doesn't swear.' What you are looking to find is what you do want, rather than what you don't.

You might like to write down your 'perfect world' ideas here:

1. ....
2. ....
3. ....
4. ....
5. ....
6. ....
7. ....

8. ....

9. ....

10. ....

These points should now form the basis for your expect-ations. Although we don't live in a perfect world, in which children always behave perfectly, there is no harm at all in setting our expectations this high.

Once you've established what your expectations are in the best of all possible situations, you should then move on to decide how fully you expect your child actually to fulfil these expectations. Your expectations should always be the same, as far as possible, although you must be able to be flexible when it is necessary. Keeping your expectations consistent will help you achieve the certainty that is so important for good behaviour management.

Making your expectations clear

As you've seen throughout this book, getting good behaviour is all about making it clear exactly what you want. In addi-tion to establishing for yourself the behaviour you want, you must also share the secret with your children. There are a number of ways that you might do this.

■ *Winging it* In reality, most of us will tend to set our expectations as we go along, responding to inappropriate behaviour by clamping down on it when it happens. There's no harm in 'winging it', so long as you can quickly establish what you want in each situation and immediately make your wishes clear to your child. So it is that the first time your child asks to watch an adult televi-sion programme, you make it clear that she will not be allowed do this and let her know why she cannot. Once you have set the expectation, you must then stick with it every time your child wants to push at this boundary in the future.

■ *Setting the expectations early* Rather than waiting and responding to poor or inappropriate behaviour, you might instead choose to sit down with your child or chil-dren and go through what you want. When you do this, please bear in mind that children find it hard to retain lots of information at once. Often they will need to experience the poor behaviour and its consequences to be able to keep it in their minds. In fact, they will usually need to misbehave a number of times, and see how their parents respond, before they can actually retain the expectation that you have set. Bear in mind, too, that you will need to limit the amount of expectations that you set at once. See the point below for some more thoughts on this.

■ *Actions speak louder than words* The majority of our expectations will be demonstrated through what we do, and what we expect our children to do. As I've already stressed, you are providing a role model for your child at all times, and she will be constantly picking up on the way you behave. You cannot set an expectation that she will not bite her nails, if she sees you doing exactly this day after day! Many of your expectations will be drummed in by what you do from the very earliest days with your child. For instance, if you always feed your child at the table, rather than in front of the television, then she will see this as the natural thing to do, and is less likely to question it.

■ *Limiting your expectations* As a teacher, I'm well aware that I can only give a small number of instructions at once if I'm going to expect them to be understood and followed. The maximum limit seems to be about three – I like to think of this as one for each ear, and one for the mouth. If you do decide to preset your expectations, then try giving a maximum of three instructions at once, perhaps starting out with what you see to be the three most important expectations of all. Once you are sure that your child has understood these and taken them on board, you could then introduce the next three ideas.

■ *Setting targets* Children (and indeed adults) do find it much easier to behave appropriately if they have something to aim for. Setting targets for our children helps encourage them to do as we wish. For instance, if you are faced with a child who doesn't like to eat vegetables, you might set a target to help encourage her to eat at least a little. Your target could be one mouthful of vegetables for every three mouthfuls of the rest of her food. Make sure that your child is likely to achieve the targets, otherwise you simply set her and yourself up for failure. You can then gradually make the targets more difficult, until your expectation of very high quality behaviour is met.

- *Giving rewards* Once you have set your targets, you can introduce some positive reinforcement. This can be done by the use of rewards when your child does stick to your expectations. For example, you could set up the expectation that your child will tidy her room, then reward this behaviour when she does live up to what you want. Chapter 7 deals in lots of detail with the whole area of rewards and sanctions.

- *Using 'I want' statements* Telling your children what you want makes it very clear to them what your expectations are. I like to use what I call 'I want . . .' statements to do this. When you are explaining your expectation of behaviour to your child, tell her exactly what you require by saying 'I want you to . . .'. Try to focus on positive behaviours as much as you can, although clearly at times you will need to say 'I want you to stop doing . . .'.

Structures

One of the key ways in which you can encourage good behaviour is by setting up structures for your child. In this section I'll explain exactly how you can go about doing this. The structures that I talk about include ideas such as having clear expectations, applying them consistently, setting the boundaries for your child and also creating routines.

Have you ever noticed how, when they are thrown into an unfamiliar situation or setting, your children will often behave badly? Of course, some children are more adaptable then others, but most young people (and indeed most adults) do like to know what to expect. Our children get used to specific things happening at specific times. These patterns help them cope with a complex and confusing world, and this is particularly important for very young children.

The structures that I discuss in this section are important for a number of reasons:

- *Giving cues* Having a clear and consistent pattern to the day gives the child cues to show what is going to happen to her next. For example, this might mean having a bedtime routine of bath, milk, story then sleep. Because the child knows what to expect, it is easier for her to behave in the appropriate way.

- *Giving clarity* Patterns and routines help you to make it clear what you are expecting the child to do. They show her how you want her to behave so that she can comply easily. These structures help reinforce your expectations, without the need for you to talk about the correct behaviour over and over again.

- *Giving consistency* If you do have a set pattern to your day, this will help you to be consistent in the way that you react to your child's behaviour. As well as your child knowing what to expect, you will also have a very clear idea of what you want at any particular time.

Of course each person reading this book will have his or her own ideas about how much structure is required or enjoyable in life. Some of us are happy to lead flexible, even chaotic lives, and there's absolutely nothing wrong with that. The issue is that, once you have children, then you will need to give at least a little structure to their world even if you don't particularly want it in your own life. The key is finding a good balance between too much or too little structure.

There are various points for and against a highly structured or loosely structured approach. Considering these points will help you decide how much structure you want or need to give to your own child's life.

Highly structured

For
- Gives a strong feeling of security.
- Offers very clear structures and patterns for behaviour.
- Tends to encourage a clear and consistent approach from parents.

Against

■ The child might prove less adaptable when routines are changed.

■ She might not know how to behave if the normal routine is broken.

■ It can mean less flexibility when managing behaviour.

Loosely structured

For

■ Encourages the child to be flexible and adaptable.

■ The child is able to cope when routines are broken.

■ Helps the parents apply more flexibility to dealing with behaviour.

Against

■ Less feeling of security and clarity for the child.

■ The child might have less understanding of the parent's expectations.

■ Tends to lead to less clarity and consistency from the parents.

What structures should I set?

Not everyone reading this book will agree about the value of structures and routines. You might prefer to respond to your child on a more ad hoc basis, simply reacting to the way that she behaves each day. As I've said, there is no real harm in having a less structured approach to life. However, if you are experiencing behaviour problems with your child, then you might find that adding more routine to her life does help.

There are various structures that you can set for your child, to help her understand how you want her to behave. These structures can be put in place right from the earliest stage. Remember that you will have to adapt the routines you build with your child as she gets older. For instance, when she is very young, she might have three or even four naps a day. As she gets older these nap times will obviously change and eventually she will not need to sleep during the day at all.

- *Structures for the day* This will include the routines that you set up for your child. It might mean having certain times of the day when you play with your child, other times when she naps, and other times when she must entertain herself or help you with the housework. With a school-age child, you might set up a structure for when and where she does her homework in the evenings.

- *Structures for the week* You can also start to structure your week, so your child learns the pattern of the days. With a pre-school child you could have certain days that you go out of the house, for instance to do the shopping, to go swimming, to toddler group or other organized activities. Once children start school, the weekly structure during term time obviously becomes that of going to school on week days. However, you still have the chance to set up a structure for the weekends and the holidays.

- *Structures for behaviour* These are the most important structures of all when it comes to managing behaviour. What you are basically trying to do is to set the limits for your child, to make it totally clear about the boundaries within which she must stay. Remember that you will need structures for when your child has behaved well, in addition to some for when she has misbehaved. These positive structures might include set rewards for particular examples of good behaviour.

What are boundaries and why do we need them?

Boundaries are another word for the limits or structures we give to our children, and they link very closely to the expectations discussed above. I like to use the image of a box to explain what boundaries are. Imagine that your child is inside a large box. Within this area are all the things that she is allowed to do, indeed all the things that you actually want her to do (your expectations of her behaviour). When your child tries to push at the boundaries, this is the equivalent of trying to step outside the box. The outer edges of the box are where the boundaries lie. Every time she tries to step out of the box you have created for her, you need to encourage her to go back inside. You might do this by making the consequences of her behaviour clear, for instance by using sanctions. Of course, your focus should be mainly on encouraging the right behaviour through more positive approaches.

Setting boundaries means showing your child what you want her to do. You are effectively telling her that you find certain behaviours acceptable (inside the box), and others unacceptable (outside the box). As with every aspect of raising our children, the boundaries that you set will differ according to the way that you believe children should behave. It is finding the dividing line between acceptable and unacceptable behaviour that is so important.

Making these decisions is not easy. To give an example, you will need to decide for yourself what you consider to be acceptable and unacceptable language. Your ideas about which words are not allowed will be subject to your own personal choices. Clearly, the 'f' word and other strong swear words lie far outside the boundaries of allowable behaviour, whether said accidentally or particularly if spoken to another person. However, do you mind if your child says 'oh bum!' if she gets frustrated about something? These are choices only you can make for your child.

For our society to work, boundaries are absolutely essential. For instance, imagine if there were no limits set on good and bad behaviour at school. If the students were allowed to mess around as and when they wanted, there would be very little chance of learning taking place. Similarly, if there were no boundaries in society as a whole about what is or is not allowed, there would be far more crime and disorder.

How do I set boundaries?

- *Let your child 'in on the secret'* As soon as she is old enough to understand, spend time talking to your child about your boundaries. Explain to her what you do want, as well as what you don't. For the younger child, your boundaries will be made clear by the way that you react to her behaviour, and the patterns that you set up for her.

- *Provide a role model* There is no point in setting boundaries that you don't follow yourself, and expecting your child to comply. As a parent you provide a role model for your child. You can't tell her not to do something, then continue to do it yourself. Similarly, if you do something as a matter of course, then you can expect your child to pick up the same behaviours. This applies to those good and bad habits that all of us have. For instance the positive (or negative) role model that you provide might include:

- the type of language you use
- the sorts of food you eat
- the type and amount of television you watch
- the way that you treat other people – family, friends and others
- the way that you take care of your personal hygiene
- the way in which you keep your home

- *React consistently to 'out of the box' behaviour* I'm happy to repeat the idea of consistency, because it is so important in establishing good behaviour. Every time your child steps outside the 'box' of the boundaries you have set, push her back inside by making the limits clear. You might do this by giving a sanction, or preferably by making the right behaviour more attractive. Keep the signals you send clear and consistent, and your child will eventually get the message.

What boundaries should I set?

There is a whole range of boundaries that you could potentially set for your child. Much will depend on your own views of what is appropriate behaviour, and also on the type of parent you are or hope to be. Here are some examples of boundaries that I might establish both in the classroom and in the home, and some examples of both 'in the box' (allowed) and 'out of the box' (not allowed) behaviours:

- The use of appropriate language at all times.
    - in the box: speaking politely to others
    - out of the box: swearing (note: what you mean by a 'swear word' needs to be defined)
- The proper treatment of others, whether parents, brothers and sisters, friends, family, classmates or simply other people that the child meets.

- in the box: sharing, saying 'please' and 'thank you'
- out of the box: snatching or grabbing, being violent or aggressive
- Treating possessions and places with respect.
  - in the box: keeping your room tidy, taking care of your toys
  - out of the box: vandalism, e.g. writing on walls or damaging toys

How do I enforce the boundaries?

- *Use of rewards* There are two basic ways of enforcing the boundaries you have set. Your main focus should be on the use of rewards to encourage positive behaviour. The message to your child is: if you do 'good behaviour x', you will receive 'reward y'.

- *Use of sanctions* The other option is the use of sanctions. As soon as your child tries to push outside the boundaries, you should immediately make it clear what the consequences will be. If your child sees that you mean business, then she may well stop the misbehaviour rather than earning the sanction.

- *Make them attractive* If you can make staying inside the box more attractive than leaving it, then the battle will be half won. There are various ways that you might make complying attractive. You might use heaps of praise to draw attention to positive behaviour; you could set targets to bring out the competitive streak in your child.

Positivity

The word 'positivity' sums up for me the attitude that you need to take if you want to get and maintain good behaviour from your children. The secret to getting what you want is to make it so attractive that it is by far the best option for your child to choose. Rather than focusing on what you don't want, you keep your mind on what you do want.

It can be hard to remain positive, particularly when you are faced with repeated examples of poor behaviour. I know as a teacher, that when I have to teach a class that always tries my patience, I can quickly get ground down by this and a negative feeling can start to take hold. However, if you can try as hard as possible to retain this positivity, then you will eventually overcome the negative behaviours and replace them with positive ones instead. Here are some tips about how to achieve positivity:

- *Expect the best* As I've said before, the higher the standards we set for our children, the better they are likely to behave. Of course this does not mean that you should set the standards impossibly high. On the other hand, if you show your children that you have complete belief in their ability to do well, then they will generally try to live up to your expectations.

- *Look for the best* As well as expecting the best from your child, you should also aim to look for the best in everything she does. When we're dealing with difficult behaviour on a daily basis, it is all too easy to slip into a negative frame of mind. Try instead looking for the good things that your child is doing, even if this is as simple as getting dressed in the morning on time for school without complaining or making a scene.

- *Praise the best* Always praise your child when she is doing the right thing, no matter how tempting it is to ignore her, breathing a silent 'phew'. If she does make a stride in behaving much better, then lavish vast amounts of praise on her, and give her a really good reward. This will show her the benefits of doing what you want, and encourage her to do it again.

Energy

If you're anything like me, you probably find being a parent pretty exhausting. I thought I'd done some tough jobs in my time, but until I became a mum I didn't really know what hard work meant. Some days it seems like you're on the go from the moment the day starts, right through into the night. Even when your child is asleep, there is still that worry in the back of your mind that you might get a wake-up call.

Being a parent requires huge amounts of energy. There's all the day-to-day work that children cause, such as feeding, washing up, laundry, housework, helping with homework. But there's also the input that you make into dealing with their behaviour, and in helping them to learn. If you can add a certain spark of energy to the way that you deal with your children, then it's almost inevitable that you will build a better relationship with them.

The energy that is so vital to being a parent covers a range of areas. You might be offering your child:

- *Enthusiasm* Noting how well she has done, perhaps in learning a new skill, or in behaving particularly well. Being enthusiastic about the simple things, such as the way that she helps you in dressing her, by putting up her arm to go through the sleeve.

- *Encouragement* Using an energetic tone to encourage her in her behaviour or in her play. For instance you might be showing her how to complete a jigsaw and encouraging her when she makes an attempt to copy you.

- *Excitement* Getting excited when she does something new, again either in her learning or in the way that she behaves. This might mean showing your excitement when a young child tries to say a new word or being delighted when she gets a good mark and comment on some schoolwork.

- *Engaging* Using your energetic attitude to parenting to find new and interesting ways to engage her. For example putting on a voice and making teddy 'speak' to her about how well she is doing.

When your aim is to encourage good behaviour, all of these approaches and attitudes will help you. You should particularly try to use these when your child is being good, to encourage a repeat of this type of behaviour. I know how hard it is to maintain this attitude with your children, especially when you're feeling tired, or when they have been trying your patience to the maximum, but if you can then you will reap the benefits in better behaviour.

How do I communicate my energy?

There are various ways that you can demonstrate your energy to your child. You will do this by using all the approaches described above. Your energy will mainly be communicated through the way that you use your voice and your face. For example, you might put an enthusiastic tone into your voice when you see her doing something well, or give her a big smile when she pleases you.

How do I find this energy?

At this point you might be thinking: 'How the hell am I supposed to find all this energy? I work five days a week, do the school run, keep the house clean and organized, do the shopping, help my kids with their homework, deal with three squabbling children at once. By the end of the day I'm too knackered even to pretend to have any energy left.'

As a parent and someone who runs my own business, I can assure you that I fully understand this feeling. Here are some tips to help you find a bit more energy to deal with your children:

- *Don't take on too much* If you are a full-time mother or father, it might be tempting to get involved in lots of different activities alongside your parenting role: PTA, voluntary work, running a playgroup, helping out with reading at your child's school and so on. Among all these commitments, do try not to take on too much, or your energy levels will dip and the quality of the time you spend with your children will suffer. Similarly, if you work full time then you will need to avoid taking on too many commitments outside of your normal working hours, or you risk running yourself into the ground.

- *Find a balance* There is a very delicate balance to be found between being a parent and being a person. Even though we love our children dearly, we are not just mothers or fathers, we are friends, lovers and so on as well. For instance, if you find being at home with your children all week draining, then why not try and organize some part-time childcare so that you can work one day a week? Although this might not actually give you much of a financial reward, it will give you some time away from the home and allow you to see yourself as a person as well as a parent.

■ *Learn to prioritize* As a teacher, I know that it is completely impossible to do everything that needs to be done, because in a job that has no real limits, there will always be something that needs doing. The same applies to being a parent. If your child needs more of your attention, then forget the hoovering and spend time playing with her. Work out what really needs to be done, and what can wait or conveniently be 'forgotten'. Learn to accept when 'good enough' is good enough.

■ *Get your kids to help* Asking your children to help you out with some of the more mundane tasks will allow you to keep your energy for what really counts. In the long run, giving our children responsibility for keeping their rooms tidy, washing up after their meals, doing a bit of hoovering, helping with the shopping and so on will help them become more capable and able people.

■ *Use your support networks* As a parent, there are options for getting some support when you need it. If you have friends or family close by, these people can give you some 'time out' (see below) when you're at the end of your tether. Even if you don't, there are still ways in which you can get some support: from toddler groups and playgroups, to paid childcare or children's playcentres and activity holidays.

■ *Take some 'time out' occasionally* Being a parent really is a full time job – 24 hours a day, 7 days a week. If at all possible, do try to take some 'time out' occasionally, even if this is only an hour to yourself to read your favourite magazine in peace. You need this time to refresh yourself, to recharge your batteries so that you have the energy necessary for staying positive as a parent.

The energy equation

I'd like to end this section by talking about what I call the 'energy equation'. This equation helps to answer the question that I dealt with above, which is 'where on earth am I meant to get this energy from?' It is of course up to the individual parent how much energy he or she wants to put into bringing up children. There will be times when you have very little energy available, and when you would rather let your child whinge than spend another second playing with her. Don't feel guilty when these feelings strike – we are not robots with endless supplies of energy and enthusiasm.

However, it is worth considering the energy equation when these feelings of tiredness do hit home. The equation can be summed up as follows:

> The more effort you put into taking a positive attitude, and dealing with your children with as much energy and enthusiasm as you can, the less energy you will need to spend on dealing with poor behaviour. In the long run, putting the energy you have into these positive approaches will mean less need to work hard in dealing with negative behaviour in the future.

Although it's hard work at first, putting in the effort from the start will eventually pay dividends, I promise.

Communication

Often, problems with behaviour happen because parents fail to communicate properly with their children. We might feel that we are giving one message, and then be surprised when our child seems not to understand. There are various ways in which we might fail to communicate properly. It could be that you are:

- failing to communicate exactly what you want from your child
- not explaining properly about the consequences of poor behaviour
- failing to put across the positive benefits of good behaviour
- not making yourself clear in the way that you talk to your children
- not making full use of body language and facial expressions to clarify your meaning

■ failing to give clear and unequivocal instructions or commands

Failures in communication can lead to a number of problems, and in turn to misbehaviour. Your child might feel a sense of unfairness, when you apply a sanction that has not been properly explained. Here are some tips about communicating properly with your child. You can find lots more detail about sending signals to your child in Chapter 6.

■ *State what you want in a positive way* When you're communicating your requirements to your child, you need to state clearly what you want in a positive manner. Often, when faced by misbehaviour we will fall into nagging or asking pointless questions that don't require an answer, rather than actually stating what it is we really want. Consider the difference between the following clear/positive and unclear/negative requests:
  ■ *Clear/positive* 'I want you to show mum how clever you are by finishing off your homework in exactly five minutes. Ready, steady, go!'
  ■ *Unclear/negative* 'Why haven't you finished your homework yet? I can't believe you're messing me around again. I told you last night that you weren't going to watch TV until you'd finished, and here you go again not doing what I tell you.'
  ■ *Clear/positive* 'I want you to stop hitting Katy over the head with that toy right now. Come on, let's see how grown-up and sensible you can be!'
  ■ *Unclear/negative* 'Why are you hitting your sister again, haven't I told you a million times not to do that? If you do it again, I'm going to smack your bottom.'
■ *Be willing to listen* Often, when we experience poor behaviour, we will talk at our children in an attempt to drum into them what we mean. After a while, the child will tend to phase out, and not really hear what you're saying. Sometimes you need to take a step backwards from the situation, and show that you are willing to listen to your child's thoughts and feelings. This doesn't necessarily mean that you will give in to what your child

wants, but sometimes just listening and acknowledging her viewpoint will be enough.

■ *Talk about the behaviour* If it seems appropriate, when your child does something 'wrong', let her talk to you about it. If she can learn to communicate some of the reasons why she did what she did, this will help you to plan ways of getting better behaviour in the future.

■ *Find ways of communicating* Try to use a whole range of ways of communicating with your child. You will already be using lots of these, but do try to extend your forms of communication as far as you can. You can find lots of details about this in the next chapter. Here are a few ideas to get you started:

   ■ your voice – what you say and how you say it

   ■ your face – the way you use your eyes, mouth, etc.

   ■ your body – the way you stand and the physical actions that you take

   ■ your interaction – the way you interact with your child and with the space around you

Training

Finally, getting good behaviour and two-way respect is all about training your children. You can't expect a very young child to understand what you want from her, but if you can set up the correct behaviours for her, she will usually be able to take these behaviours on board. Much of the poor behaviour that we experience as parents comes about as a result of conflict over the day-to-day things that we need our children to do. As you'll see below, a bit of early training can mean these 'battle grounds' never turn into areas where difficult behaviour is an issue.

In the film *Kindergarten Cop*, Arnold Schwarzenegger plays a police officer working undercover in a primary school. At first he has huge problems – the children basically run rings around him, getting away with their poor behaviour because he has not set the limits for them. Not knowing much about teaching, he falls back on what he does know – the way that police recruits are trained. By the end of the film his class of

young children are lining up in single file, marching properly, giving him their silent attention, and putting away
equipment in military fashion.

Just as with this film, your training should focus on the
positive behaviours you do want, rather than on any thought
of negative behaviour or sanctions. If you can set your child
up to succeed in behaving in the right way, and keep
reinforcing these positive ideas, then hopefully you should
find that many of these areas never become an issue between
you. Start your training early, with the easiest parts of each
task, moving on to give more difficult requests as your child
gets older.

What training should I give?

Although you might not be aware of it, you will already be
training your child in the behaviours that you want, through
showing her your expectations on a consistent basis. There
are various common 'battle grounds' between parents and
children, areas where problems often occur. The use of early
training can be of great help in getting these things right, and
consequently in getting the behaviour that you want.

Here are some questions about what your expectations
might be in two of these traditional battlegrounds. Answer-
ing these questions will help you start to understand what
you want when it comes to training your child in your
expectations of her behaviour. Bear in mind that your
expectations will probably change over time, as your child
grows up.

Eating

■ *What happens before meals?* Is she asked to help prepare
the meal or to lay the table? Is she expected to wash her
hands before eating?

■ *Where does she eat?* Is this at the table, in a seat or on the
sofa watching the television?

■ *Who does she eat with?* Will you eat as a family or with
one parent present to supervise? Will she eat with any
siblings, or will meal times be separate?

■ *How does she eat 'properly'?* Will she be expected to stay in her seat until everyone has finished eating? What will happen if she misbehaves, for example throwing food on the floor or refusing to eat her vegetables?

■ *What do you want her to eat?* Which sorts of food will you encourage her to eat, and which foods will be given less often? Do you set an example for her by eating these 'good' foods yourself? Will all your children eat the same meals, or will you allow them some choice over what they want to eat?

■ *What happens after eating?* Will your child help to clear the table and perhaps wash up as well? Will she be expected to sit still for a while after her meal, to let her food go down, or can she head off to play immediately?

Sleeping

■ *What time does she go to bed?* Is there a set time, or are you going to be flexible about this? Does she have a say in what time she goes to sleep? Do all your children go to bed at the same time, or can the older siblings stay up later?

■ *What is the bedtime routine?* Does she have a set routine, for example bath, drink, story, bed? Is she allowed to watch television in her room? Do you switch the light off or is she allowed to do this for herself? Are there any times when you allow her to break the routine, and what circumstances does this include?

■ *What happens after going to bed?* Is she expected to stay in her room for the night, or can she come into your room or your bed if she wants, for instance if she's feeling unwell? What time is she allowed to get up or come into your room in the morning?

How do I train my child?

■ *Make it a challenge* Young children love to be given challenges. Set up your 'training' to take advantage of this. Make doing the right thing, and doing it as well as possible, a challenge for your child to complete. At all times, explain to your child how well she is doing already, but also how much better you know she can do in the future.

For some ideas about how to make the training a challenge, see the points below about tidying the bedroom.

■ *Set limits* If you set your child a target to aim for, this will often encourage her to reach for the positive behaviour that you want. For instance, you might set limits that are to do with completing something in a certain time or doing a particular amount of something. To give a specific example, if you want your child to tidy up her room, you could set her a time limit of five minutes, or you could ask her to compete alongside her brothers or sisters to see who can finish first.

■ *Make it seem like a game* If the 'training' seems like a fun game, rather than just one more demand, then it is far more likely that your children will comply. For instance, in the example of tidying the bedroom above, you might set it up as a competition between siblings. To do this you might use a stopwatch, have a big prize for the winner and runner-up prizes for the others, and say 'ready, steady, go' before they start. You could then keep reminding them how much time has gone as they hurry to complete the task. This helps to make the task more fun and concrete, focusing your children and encouraging them to have fun while they work.

■ *Use rewards* Once you have set a limit and a challenge, you can then offer your child or children a reward for completing the task. Tell her all about the exciting reward that she will receive when she has finished. Make the reward something that your child wants to earn, perhaps discussing her preferred reward with her before she begins the task.

■ *Create fictions* As we saw in the example of the film *Kindergarten Cop*, children respond very well to fictions. In the film, Schwarzenegger creates the fiction that the children are police recruits, and as part of their training they must put the positive behaviours into place. Taking the example of your children tidying their bedrooms, you might tell them that they are going to be detectives, and hide a couple of 'clues' under all the mess. This will encourage them to tidy up in a careful and focused way.

■ *Keep practising* Getting the training right will take lots of practice. You can bring some fun into this practice, by setting the practice up as a kind of game. To give you just one idea, if you're brave enough you might actually tell your child that she can spend a day getting her room as messy as possible, so that she can practise her tidying-up skills.

SIX

Sending Signals

We are all sending signals to our children all the time, whether we realize it or not. I've already talked about how proper communication is really important in getting your children to behave well. In this chapter you'll find much more information about how you can communicate with your children in the most effective way. As a teacher, I communicate with classes of 30 or more children, and I have to make very clear use of my face, voice and body to ensure that I get what I want. In this chapter I pass on some of the best tips and strategies that I have learnt through my years of working with children of all different ages.

There are lots of ways of communicating with your child. In this chapter I divide these ways up into verbal and non-verbal signals. The most obvious way of communicating is simply by talking to him about what you want. It's not just *what* you say, though, it's also about the *way* that you actually say it. I look below at how you can improve the quality of the verbal signals that you send to your child.

As well as communicating with our voices, we can also

communicate in other ways. These non-verbal signals include the way that we use our bodies, the way that we use the space, our use of different levels and so on. Often, these non-verbal signals send a much more powerful message to our children than simply talking to them. Bear in mind that you can use all these different types of signals to send positive messages to your child, rather than focusing on the more negative types of communication.

By making small changes to the signals that you send, you can tell your child whether he is behaving in the right or wrong way. When it comes to dealing with poor behaviour, you can also use these signals to show different degrees of right and wrong. For instance, sometimes a child will mis-behave in a really serious way, whereas at other time the mis-behaviour will only be minor. The signals that we send to our children will help us indicate just how negative or positive their behaviour is.

Verbal signals

Most of us turn to using our voices when we want to com-municate with our children. Of course this is not possible if the child doesn't yet understand the words that we are using. You might have noticed how your young child appears to understand what you're saying, even though he isn't yet speaking. He may in fact understand a great deal more than you realize, but you will also be communicating in other, more subtle ways. For instance your tone of voice and also the non-verbal signals you are giving will help to make your meaning clear.

In this section I'm going to look at the verbal signals we give our children. First of all I'll look at the way we actually use our voices, for instance the volume and tone that we put into our voices. I'll then go on to look at what we actually say, examining the best ways in which to communicate through speaking with your child.

Using your voice

When we use our voices to communicate with our children, we tend to focus in on what we are saying, rather than on the way we are saying it. It really is worth becoming more aware of how you use your voice, though, as this can have a big impact on the quality of your communication with your child. Here are some tips that will help you become more aware of the way that you use your voice:

- *Learn to hear yourself* If you can learn to hear yourself when you're talking to your child, this will help you use your voice more effectively. You'll probably find that the way you imagine you sound is very different in reality. There are several ways that you can hear yourself. These include:

    - asking someone else (perhaps the other parent or a relative) to tell you how your voice sounds when you're dealing with your child

    - stepping 'outside' yourself to try and hear how you sound to your child

    - if you're brave enough, taping or video-recording yourself to get a 'warts and all' view

- *Remember that children hear differently* Do try to remember that children are smaller than us. This means that they will hear us differently to the way we sound to ourselves or to other adults. For instance, what sounds like a normal volume level to you may in fact sound very loud to your children.

- *Learn to hear your child* As well as learning to hear yourself, do train yourself to listen to the signals that your child is sending you through his voice. You might notice that he sounds stressed, angry or sad. The sound in his voice will help you understand his emotional state, and subsequently to deal with him in the most appropriate way.

When it comes to using our voices, there are four main areas to think about. These are volume, speed, tone and emotion. I give you some more thoughts about these below, including tips on how to use your voice effectively. In addition to these four areas, I look at the part singing and making other noises can play in encouraging better behaviour.

Volume

There are lots of ways that we can use the volume of our voices to help us send signals to our children. You might:

- make your voice louder to get your child's attention, or to show anger
- make your voice quieter to calm your child or to show that you're unhappy

You can use the volume of your voice to manage behaviour. Try some of the following ideas to see how they work for you:

- raising the volume slowly, rather than going straight to shouting
- being 'quiet and deadly' rather than 'loud and angry'
- making a sudden change in the volume of your voice to show how you're feeling
- combining a loud volume with a single-word command, such as 'Stop!' or 'No!' This can be surprisingly effective, but should not be over-used

Of course, within the subject of volume comes the whole idea of shouting. You'll find a separate section below devoted to this subject.

Speed

Again, you can use the speed of your words to help you manage your children's behaviour. You might:

- talk slowly to calm a situation down
- make quick changes in the speed of your voice
- use different speeds within a sentence

When it comes to the speed of your voice, remember the following:

- we often talk much faster than we realize, which makes it hard for our children to understand what we're saying

■ don't assume that just because you've said something once, it will be heard and understood

■ try slowing down the speed of your voice a lot, particularly when you are giving instructions

■ try speeding up your voice to show excitement, approval or pleasure, or to get your child's attention

Tone

The tone with which we speak can be a very powerful way of sending signals to our children. You might:

■ use an interested and excited tone of voice to show your approval of good behaviour

■ use a sharp tone to show your disapproval

■ put a soft, calming tone into your voice to cool down a situation

■ make a sudden change in tone to demonstrate your changing emotions

Here are some tips about using tone, gathered from years of working with children in the classroom.

■ the younger the child, the more you will need to exaggerate your tone of voice to help him understand what you want

■ at first, you might feel as though you sound a bit stupid doing this, but you will notice how it really does have an effect on your child's behaviour

■ try combining tone of voice with the speed at which you talk to increase the effect. For instance, use a soft tone with a slow speed to calm your child down

Emotion

The way that our voices sound will often give away our inner feelings. Bear the following points in mind to help you control your emotions:

■ when you're dealing with a difficult situation, try hard to keep your voice unemotional

- as with tone, exaggerate the emotion in your voice when you are praising your child, to make it very clear how pleased you are

The following advice will help you think about the emotion that you put in your voice, and adapt it to improve your child's behaviour.

- when we're annoyed or angry, these emotions can very easily be heard in our voices
- if your child sees that he is able to wind you up, this might give him an incentive to misbehave again
- your voice might also betray a lack of confidence, for instance a nervous emotion coming through in your voice
- try to split up your inner feelings from the emotion that can be heard in your voice

Singing and other noises

As well as communicating through normal speaking, we can also make effective use of singing and other vocal noises when dealing with our children's behaviour. These are particularly useful as forms of distraction. This might sound a bit strange, but it's actually surprisingly effective! Here are a few ideas to get you started:

- sing your child's name over and over again when he's upset
- whistle to your child to distract him when he's crying
- make animal noises to get your child's attention (and do the actions as well if you enjoy a bit of play acting!)
- try using your voice to trill, beep or in a variety of ways to distract a baby
- combine singing, tone of voice and emotion together to really delight your child
- if you can, try using different regional or international accents to talk to your child – this will amuse him and will certainly gain his attention

What to say

Learning to communicate effectively is not just about how we talk, but also about what we actually say. It is tempting to believe that we can talk to our children in the same way that we might talk to adults. However, do remember that your child is only a relative beginner when it comes to language, even when he is nearing his teenage years. You have been using language for many years: your child has only recently started, and his vocabulary is still relatively limited. The tips below will help you frame what you say in the most effective way.

- *Keep it simple* When you're communicating with your child, do make sure that you communicate using simple words and structures. Keep it in your mind that your child is only a relative beginner in understanding how language works. Try not to use complicated words or difficult sentence structures, as these will make it difficult for your child to understand exactly what you mean.

- *Talk properly* Having said that you should 'keep it simple', I do not mean that you should use baby language when talking with your child. In fact, the best way to teach our children to speak is to use pretty much a normal vocabulary with them. However, when it comes to dealing with behaviour your aim is to be as clear as you possibly can. For this reason, if you can give simple instructions in plain language, your child is more likely to do what you want.

- *Keep it short* Adults find it relatively easy to have a long conversation, one in which we speak for a while before giving someone else a turn. We are able to keep quite a large quantity of language in our minds at any one time, without needing to see the words written down. The same is not true for children. Keep your instructions or comments short – that way your child will be able to retain what you have said.

- *Stick to the '3 at a time' rule* Following on from the point above, it is my experience that children can generally only hold onto around three instructions at any one time. If you reel off a long list of demands to your child, then it should be no surprise to you when he fails to remember what you have said. Sticking to the '3 at a time' rule will help you limit the amount of verbal information you give to your child at any one time.

■ *Use statements rather than questions* When you're dealing with behaviour issues, try to focus on stating exactly what you want, rather than asking for it. Although this is only a subtle change in speech, it can actually make quite a difference to the way that your child reacts. This means that, rather than asking 'Why are you doing that when I've told you not to?' you should state 'I want you to stop doing that now, please.'

■ *Use repetition* It is easy to assume that because you have said something once, your child should be able to understand and obey. However, it will often be necessary to use repetition to ensure that your child has actually understood. You might repeat a potential sanction for continued misbehaviour. Remember too that you should repeat what you say when praising your child, to ensure that he has taken your praise on board. This is particularly so in a busy household with a number of noisy children who might make it difficult for any one child to hear what's going on.

■ *Use the 'broken record' technique* This is a wonderful method for getting your child's attention, that is widely used by teachers, but which can also be very effective in the home. The 'broken record' technique involves starting a sentence over and over again, until you have the attention you require. So it is that you might say 'Ben, I want you to . . .' and then you notice that Ben is clearly not listening. At this point you would repeat 'Ben, I want you to . . .' until he gives you his attention.

■ *Use his name* I was once given a wonderful quote, which I always try to bear in mind when I'm working with children. It goes like this: 'The sweetest sound to any child is the sound of his own name.' Your child's name is all part of what makes him a unique individual. This is one of the earliest words he will have heard, over and over again. Make sure that you use your child's name to get his attention, for instance when you want to praise or sanction him.

- *Use cues* In the classroom, I make a point of using cues when I am giving instructions to my class. For instance, when I ask a question I might start by saying 'Put your hand up if you can tell me . . .'. By giving this cue for the correct behaviour, I prevent the children shouting out the answer, and instead focus them on the approach that I do want. You can use these cues with your child in the home, too, for instance saying 'Look at me please' before you begin to talk with your child.

- *Be positive* At every opportunity, try to find ways of stressing the positive with your child when you talk with him. Learn to anticipate good behaviour, rather than expecting things to go wrong, particularly when you are asking him to do something. For instance, if you wanted your child to do the washing up, you might introduce the activity by saying 'You are so good at washing up, and you're so helpful to mummy all the time. Shall we do the washing up together, or would you like to show me how grown up you are by doing it on your own?' Set your child up for success by using positive statements and challenges as often as you can. Similarly, aim to focus mainly on the use of positive language with your child, including words such as:

  - clever
  - brilliant
  - great
  - fantastic
  - excellent

- *Be enthusiastic* It's worth thinking about how you can combine what you say with how you say it, especially when your aim is to encourage good behaviour. Remember to use tone of voice, speed, and so on in conjunction with positive language to enthuse and encourage your child.

- *Set targets* The use of targets really is an excellent way of getting the behaviour you want from your child. We all respond well when we have a goal for which to aim. You might set both short and long-term targets for your child, for instance a short-term target to finish his homework,

105

or a long-term target to get 50 merit marks from his teacher.

- *Pose a challenge* In order to get your child engaged with the whole idea of living up to the targets you set, you can make sticking to the targets a fun challenge. See the section on training your child in the previous chapter (pp. 94–5) for some more ideas about how to do this.

What not to say

Just as there are some things that we should bear in mind when we're thinking about what to say, there are also various things that we should avoid saying. The advice below will help stop you saying the wrong things to your child, although don't be too hard on yourself when you slip up from time to time.

- *Try not to be rude* It's all too easy for us to be rude to our children, especially when we are feeling tired or stressed. Do try your hardest not to use rude or impolite language. Remember at all times that you are setting an example to your child. If you say to him 'don't be so stupid' or tell him to 'shut up', then it should be no surprise if you hear the same words come out of his mouth in return.

- *If you swear, expect your child to swear too* As adults, we do sometimes expect to get away with behaviour that we would not consider acceptable from children. I know how often I let swear words slip out from day to day – when I hit my finger with a hammer I certainly don't go 'oh dear'. Having said this, I'm also well aware that if my children hear me swear then I can hardly get upset if I hear the same back from them. In fact, with swearing it is often the case that the bigger fuss we make about the words, the more appealing they become to our children.

- *Talk to children the same as adults* Do try to talk to your child in the same way that you would address another adult. By doing this, you will show a high level of respect for your child, and you will set the best possible example for him. There is absolutely no reason why, just because they are smaller than us, we should not treat our children with respect when we address them verbally.

■ *Avoid sarcasm* I know how easy it is for a sarcastic comment to slip out when I'm dealing with children. It's almost as though it gives us a secret weapon – we can say something that the child won't fully understand, but which makes us feel better inside. Do try not to be sarcastic as far as is humanly possible. Your child will not understand your sparkling wit, and may indeed by hurt by what you have said.

■ *Keep it short* Most of us love the sound of our own voices, and this can lead us to say far too much to our children. Sometimes we will nag on and on at them, and then are surprised when they don't really seem to have understood. The fact is, your children probably switched off halfway through your epic lecture!

■ *Be realistic* In my experience, particularly within the classroom, I have noticed that children will 'phase out' once their concentration has gone. It is hard for our children to retain lots of ideas in their heads, especially ones that they've only heard in a verbal format. Make sure that you're realistic about how much you can say to your child, and how much he will actually retain afterwards.

Shouting

We all lose our tempers sometimes, and shout at our children. (Or if you don't, you must be a saint!) Unfortunately, shouting doesn't really work as a way of dealing with misbehaviour. I understand completely why it happens, and I've done it lots of times myself, both at home and in the classroom. Whenever I have shouted, though, I've always done it with a sense that it is not really the right approach, and that I am in some way failing if I have to resort to raising my voice.

In my work as a teacher, if I were to shout at my classes on a regular basis, I would quickly damage my voice. I'm also very aware that shouting at poorly behaved children seems to encourage, rather than discourage, the confrontations that I want to avoid. I've thought long and hard about this subject over my years of working with children, and I have come to the firm conclusion that shouting really doesn't work. I've given some of my ideas about why this is below.

You might of course feel completely differently. Perhaps you believe that shouting works very well for you when you are dealing with your child. If this is the case, by all means continue to use this technique. Do have a look at some of the points I make below, though, and have a think about whether they apply to you.

Why doesn't shouting work?

- When you shout, you probably feel a little like you've lost control of yourself. If you feel this way, then your child will sense it too.

- Once the child sees you losing control, he will either:
  - take it as an incentive to misbehave again, to wind you up, or
  - get scared or upset, or
  - could become confrontational

- Shouting tends to encourage confrontational attitudes, both in the person shouting and also in the person being shouted at.

- Shouting can heighten a difficult situation, rather than calming it.

- When you shout, the sound of your voice will change, betraying your inner emotions.

- Emotions such as anger, lack of confidence or even unhappiness, will be communicated to your child, and will have an effect on his behaviour.

- When we shout we tend to lose the vital elements of tone and speed in our voices, using a single pitch instead. This damages the effectiveness of your communication with your child.

- It is harder to stay rational when you shout, because you have effectively lost at least a little control of yourself. When you become irrational, it's much harder to deal with a problematic situation.

- Finally, do think about how you feel when someone shouts at you – it's not very nice, is it? Again, remember at all times that you're modelling the correct behaviour for your child. If you shout at him, then don't be surprised if the day comes when he shouts right back at you!

Of course you probably will still want to use shouting sometimes. There will certainly be times when you shout, despite knowing inside yourself that it isn't really the best thing to do. When this does happen, please don't be too hard on yourself. A final thought on this subject – one very good tip that I've learnt during my years in the classroom is only to shout when you're not actually angry. Because you're in control, both of yourself and of your emotions, shouting can work quite effectively as a sanction in these situations.

Non-verbal signals

When I'm training other teachers in ways of managing their students' behaviour, I talk a lot about the use of 'non-verbal signals'. These are simply signals that we send to our children without using words. As well as communicating with our voices, we can also 'say' a lot without actually opening our mouths. From the earliest age, children are very adept at reading these signals. We often don't realize what signals we are sending, but others may be able to read us perfectly (often in a subconscious way), and this includes our children.

This section deals with all the different types of non-verbal signals, starting with the use of our bodies, and moving on to factors outside our immediate selves.

Why are non-verbal signals so important?

In the classroom, good teachers rely very heavily on non-verbal communication. These non-verbal signals provide us with a simple, easy and very powerful way of communicating with our students. Of course, non-verbal ways of communicating can also work very well in the home. There are lots of different reasons why these non-verbal signals are so helpful.

- *'Talking' without words* Non-verbal signals provide you with a very powerful way of showing what you want. You are effectively saying to the child that you can 'talk' to him without even opening your mouth. Of course the fact that you can communicate without words also makes these signals an excellent way of 'talking' to a child who does not yet understand language.

- *Focus on your face* From the very youngest age, your baby will start to focus on your face. This helps him to understand what you are trying to communicate to him. Although your baby might not understand what you say just yet, he will get lots of clues and cues from what your face is doing. This 'reading' of the face continues and improves as our children get older – to the point where they can read our mood without us even needing to open our mouths. The more communicative you can make your face, the better you will be able to manage your child's behaviour.

- *Giving you high status* If you can communicate your wishes without even needing to open your mouth, this gives you a very high status within a relationship. Although I don't particularly feel that we need our children to look up to us, I do believe that a child is more likely to follow your wishes if he respects the way that you interact with him.

- *Keeping it simple and effortless* Rather than having to use lots of words, and wasting our energy, non-verbal signals allow us to keep things simple and easy. For instance, you might communicate your disapproval with a raised eyebrow or a stern look, rather than a stream of complaints.

- *Easy to understand* The simplicity of non-verbal communication means that it is easy for our children to understand. There can be no confusion – no complaints that 'I didn't know what you meant'. If your child sees a frown on your face, and you click and point to him, there will be no doubt that you are not impressed with his behaviour.

- *Keeping it private* Using non-verbal communication means that you can 'talk' without giving the child an audience. Of course, this is very helpful in the classroom, where a child who has the rest of the class as an audience might be tempted to 'act up' even more. Similarly, in the home it allows us to 'talk' privately without anyone else being aware. For instance, this might mean communicating our displeasure to an older brother without his younger sister realizing. The privacy of the communication means that one sibling is less likely to realize what's going on, and consequently less likely to try and wind the other up about getting in trouble with mum or dad.

■ *Keeping it calm* When we use our voices there will always be the temptation to shout or lose control. If the child decides to answer back you can quickly get drawn into a very loud argument. On the other hand, if you encourage yourself to stick to using non-verbal signals, this will help you keep the situation calm. Because you are not using your voice, there will be no chance for you to raise it!

■ *Stopping you from nagging* When we talk, and particularly when we have to point out poor behaviour, it is all too easy to slip into having a moaning session. Nagging at our children about their behaviour is all too easy to do, but in fact it's not a very effective way of dealing with misbehaviour. In any case, after the first few seconds of hearing you nag at him, your child will probably phase out from what you are saying.

■ *Positive as well as negative* Remember that these non-verbal signals allow you to show approval as well as disapproval. In fact, you should aim to give at least three positive signals for every negative one. Positive signals might include a smile, a wink, a thumbs up sign, and so on.

■ *Several signals at once* When you are using non-verbal signals to communicate with your child, you will probably find that you actually combine a number of these signals at any one time. For instance, you might use a stern, disapproving look while standing with your arms crossed. The fact that you are using several signals at once will increase the power of the message you are sending.

Using your body

I'm going to deal with how to use your body from the top down. I'll start off by looking at how you might use the different parts of your face, and then move on to discuss how you can use the rest of your body as well. I'm going to discuss both the positive and negative signals that you can send with your body. The positive signals provide ways of showing your pleasure or approval, while the negative ones offer ways of showing that you've noted some poor behaviour or that you want the child to stop what he's doing immediately. Do remember that your aim should be to send lots of these positive signals, and to try to limit the number of negatives ones that you have to use.

Much of what I talk about here is actually natural and instinctive, and you will probably find that you use lots of non-verbal signals already. The more aware you can be about what you're doing, the more you can increase your use of the most effective signals. Do bear in mind that not all signals will be equally effective with different children. For instance, with a child who becomes aggressive quickly you might want to avoid the excessive use of eye contact, because this might make him react in a more confrontational way.

Your face

Positive signals
- making eye contact to show that you've noticed something good
- widening your eyes to show excitement or approval
- smiling (preferably with your whole face) to show that you are happy
- mouth open, eyes wide to say 'wow, aren't you clever?'
- winking at your child, with a slight smile on your face

Negative signals
- making eye contact to show that you're aware of some misbehaviour just about to happen
- frowning to show irritation or annoyance

- raising your eyebrows to say 'are you sure you want to do that?'
- using your eyes to give a 'deadly stare'. (This is a great favourite with teachers as it can silence a child or class without a single word!)

Your hands

Positive signals
- clapping your hands to show approval
- a 'thumbs up' signal to say 'well done'
- doing 'high fives' or banging fists together to show a job well done between the two of you
- a stroke or pat to show your love

Negative signals
- bringing your hands to cover your mouth to show shock
- clicking once and then pointing to say 'stop that immediately'
- hands palms down, pushing downwards to say 'calm down'
- clapping once to gain the child's attention and say 'stop'

Body language

Positive signals
- arms out towards the child, signalling 'give me a hug, you're great!'
- leaning in to show interest in what he's doing
- crouching down and getting close, again to signal your attention

Negative signals
- standing still, arms folded across your chest
- hands on hips, looking at the child with a 'deadly' stare

■ turning your back on the child – withdrawing your attention as an indication of your displeasure

Other ways of sending signals

As well as using our faces, hands and bodies to send signals, there are also some other techniques available to us. I've listed just some of these below. As you become more aware of the non-verbal ways in which you communicate, you will probably be able to add many more to the list.

■ *Using space* The position of our bodies in relation to another person can send powerful signals about what we want. For instance, you might get close to a child who is misbehaving to show that you're aware of what's going on. Alternatively, picking up a child who is playing with something dangerous, or leading him away from the area by the hand, will signal that you want him to stop.

■ *Using levels* When I want to talk to a child in the classroom, particularly when I have to deal with misbehaviour, I try to get on the same level as far as possible. This makes it easier to maintain eye contact with the child, and it also makes it clear that you know what is going on. When you do need to chat with your child, try to get down on his level, perhaps by crouching beside him or by sitting with him on the floor.

■ *Using places* We can also send some powerful signals by the use of various different places. For instance, you might use a 'naughty chair' where your child has to sit if he's done something wrong. A variation of this is using the bottom step of the stairs, or even sending the child to his room.

The power of doing nothing

Sometimes we can send a very strong message simply by doing nothing. This might mean using the 'tactical ignore' or 'blanked face' techniques described below. The key to 'doing nothing' is to learn when it is the appropriate strategy to use. You might use these approaches when:

- your child is doing something silly rather than very naughty, perhaps to get your attention

- your intervention will tend to encourage a repetition of the poor behaviour rather than discourage it

- your child knows that what he is doing is wrong, for instance where you have previously discussed the inappropriate behaviour

- where doing nothing will give your child time to consider his behaviour, and to come to the right decision of his own accord

- you simply need to regain your child's attention, but you don't want to fight to achieve this

As a teacher, I find that doing nothing is a very powerful technique within the classroom. For instance, I might be in the middle of talking to a class, when I say something that amuses them, and they all start to laugh. Now at this point I could get stressed and expect them to return their attention to me instantly. That approach, though, is a recipe for more stress than is needed. Instead, simply standing still and silent, and waiting for the class to become quiet is a much simpler and more effective way of signalling what I want.

When you're dealing with misbehaviour, don't be afraid to take a pause on occasions. This gives both you and your child time to reflect on what is happening. It gives you both the chance to calm down too, and this will help you both deal with things in a more rational way. Below you'll find some more details about two specific ways of using this approach that you might like to try with your own child.

The 'tactical ignore'

The 'tactical ignore' means ignoring minor misbehaviour as appropriate. As I've already pointed out, giving your attention for every little thing will send the wrong signals to your child. He will start to learn that if he wants your attention, all he has to do is misbehave. It's far better to give him your attention when he is doing what you want, and to learn when ignoring is the appropriate method to use. You will need to find a balance between ignoring minor misbehaviours, and letting your child get away with the more serious misdemeanours that require your attention. Again you will be making constant choices about your expectations.

The blanked face

Showing your child a totally blank face can be a very powerful technique when he misbehaves. Your blank face says 'I have no intention of responding to what you're doing, you are not getting to me in the slightest, in fact I don't even acknowledge your presence when you do that.' By withdrawing your attention in this way you send a very strong signal to your child. He is used to seeing emotion on your face – whether love or anger. The blank look takes all your attention away and replaces it with nothing.

SEVEN

Positive Praise, Positive Punishment

Two of the most powerful weapons we have in getting our children to behave as we wish are rewards and punishments. If you can learn how to use these strategies in a positive way, you will be amazed at the difference it can make to your children's behaviour. At the simplest level, a reward gives a child a reason for repeating good behaviour again – if she does she will earn the same reward again. A punishment gives her a reason not to repeat the behaviour, because she wants to avoid a repeat of the sanction.

In my years as a teacher, I've had to use both rewards and sanctions on numerous occasions. In this chapter I'm going to share with you some of the tips, strategies and secrets that

I've discovered. I look at the different types of rewards and sanctions that you might use and how best you can apply them. I also give you an outline of a plan for putting them into practice. As I've said throughout this book, do try to expect the absolute best from your children. Set your expectations high, and remember to reward your children regularly when they do what you want.

Positive praise, positive punishment

I'd like to start this chapter by explaining what the title 'positive praise, positive punishment' actually means. The following ideas sum up what I mean when I use this phrase:

- Creating a positive, rather than a negative, atmosphere in the relationship between you and your child or children.
- A focus on the behaviour that you do want, rather than on the behaviour that you don't want.
- Learning to fight against the natural temptation to focus on a poorly behaved child.
- Instead, teaching yourself to pay attention when your children are behaving well.
- Sending your children the message that the way to earn your attention is by doing the right, not the wrong, thing.
- Focusing on giving rewards, rather than on setting punishments.
- Trying to use at least three rewards to every one punishment or sanction.
- Catching your children being good as often as possible.
- When your children are good, rewarding this as quickly and as fully as you can.
- Making sure that your children are keen to earn the rewards that you give.
- When you do have to use sanctions, trying to apply them in a positive way.
- Expecting things to go right when you are dealing with your children's behaviour.

- Having an expectation that your children will do what you want.
- Acting surprised, rather than angry, when your children do misbehave.

Rewards

This first section deals with the 'positive praise' half of the equation. I've chosen to focus on this area first, to make it clear that it is much more important than punishment. In this part of the chapter, I look at how you can make rewards work for you and your children. I also examine the different types of rewards that we might use. I finish by exploring how best you can apply the rewards you decide to put into place.

Making rewards work

As a teacher, I'm well aware of how difficult it is actually to make rewards work. In order to make rewards work for you and your children in the home, try following the advice below.

- a reward will only work if a child actually wants to receive it
- different rewards will work better at different ages
- different rewards will work for different children
- find out what works best for you and your child or each of your individual children
- once you've found an effective reward, make the most of it, using it as often as is sensible
- bear in mind that any child will change over time, and this includes the rewards that will work with her. Be willing to chuck a reward away when it no longer works
- the best and most effective rewards are often free and easy to use. (See 'types of rewards' below for some ideas)
- you can set up many of life's little pleasures as a reward

rather than a right, for instance television, sweets and pocket money

■ be inventive and original about the rewards that you use. (See pp. 44–47 on being creative, for some ideas on how to do this)

Instant *v* deferred rewards

There are two basic types of reward, or gratification. A reward can either be an instant reaction to good behaviour, or it can be something that is earned over a longer period of time. When you're considering whether to use instant or deferred rewards, bear the following points in mind.

■ Using an instant reward will make an immediate connection in a child's mind between the good behaviour and the reward for it.

■ You might use a deferred reward by asking for a series of good behaviours before the reward is earned.

■ You could mark each of these good behaviours in some way, as a reminder of how well the child is doing. For instance, you could use a sticker or points system (see p. 122).

■ Instant rewards tend to be smaller, while deferred rewards might be larger, perhaps material ones (for instance a toy).

■ Very young children will not be able to sustain the connection between good behaviour and a reward that is not given immediately.

■ The older your children are, the more able they will be to understand and accept deferred gratification.

Types of rewards

Your praise

- Praise is one of most powerful rewards of all.
- Our children want us to be pleased with them.
- Praise is easy and free to give.
- Praise makes you and your child feel good.
- Catch your child doing what you want, then praise, praise, praise!
- Use words like 'brilliant', 'excellent' and 'superb'.
- You really cannot overdo the use of praise.

Treats

- Treats such as sweets, money and TV are very popular rewards.
- You can use these treats as a privilege rather than a right.
- You might reward each positive behaviour with a small amount of money, making the child 'earn' her pocket money.
- Do think about the signals that you're sending.
- For instance, do you want your child to associate sweet things with being rewarded?

Your time/your attention

- This is another very powerful reward.
- Again, it is free, although not always easy or available to give.
- Playing with your children helps them learn.
- Playing with your children should be fun!
- Give your attention when your child is behaving well, not badly.
- Offer time together (e.g. a trip out) as a 'carrot' for good behaviour.

Stars and stickers

- Stars and stickers offer a visual way of showing your approval.
- These rewards effectively 'stand for' our praise.
- A star chart can be used to record deferred rewards.
- If she achieves x number of stars, the child receives reward y.
- In my experience, children do love stickers!
- Let your child put the sticker on the chart, to make the reward even more special.

Points systems

- A system where 'points' are earned can be used to defer rewards.
- You might use coins in a jar or something similar.
- This helps make the reward visible and engaging.
- The child could earn a bigger reward for a series of points.
- This type of approach is better for the older child, who understands deferred gratification.

How to give rewards

You might think it should be a simple matter to give rewards. In fact, if you want to reward your child in the most effective way, there are a number of tips that you should follow.

- make it clear exactly why the reward is being given
- make a very clear connection between the good behaviour and the reward
- talk with your child about how this reward can be earned again
- set a target for which the child can aim to gain a further reward

■ keep your expectations high, perhaps making the target a little harder to achieve each time

A thought about distractions

You'll notice that I have emphasized throughout this book how useful distractions can be when moving a child away from poor behaviour. There will come a time, though, where you will want actually to deal with the misbehaviour, rather than simply distracting the child away from it. For instance, if a child is repeatedly throwing a tantrum when one parent leaves the room, eventually you will want her to deal with this issue herself, rather than simply being distracted from the tantrum by the other parent time after time.

It is hard to give you a specific moment when this process should begin – much will depend on your parenting style, the individual child, the particular behaviour with which you are dealing, and so on. You will know yourself when the time has come – when the child is not simply going to cry and cry and get herself worked up, and instead is going to be able to deal with the behaviour and its consequences.

Sanctions

In schools we use the word 'sanctions' to talk about punishments. There is a very good reason why this is a more appropriate word to use in the home as well. The idea is that you are not actually trying to punish your child. Instead you are aiming to sanction a particular behaviour that the child has shown. Sanctions should always be aimed at the behaviour itself, rather than the child. You are not trying to make the child feel that she has been bad, but rather that it is the behaviour that you do not want to see repeated.

Making sanctions work

Over the years as a teacher, I've had to apply sanctions on numerous occasions. Although I would always stress the need for positive approaches, there are some situations where a sanction is the best or only option. If a child has behaved in a totally inappropriate way, then she must learn that this behaviour will be punished. Hopefully, by applying the best type of sanction, and giving it in the best possible way, your child will quickly learn not to repeat the behaviour.

Here are some useful tips that will help you in getting sanctions to work with your child:

■ Try to give sanctions as infrequently as possible, although obviously use them when they are deserved.

■ Bear in mind that punishments can create a negative atmosphere, and can have a detrimental effect on the relationship between you and your children.

■ Always try to turn to more positive means instead, whenever appropriate, for instance using a distraction.

■ Alternatively, try rewarding the good behaviour of a sibling instead to show your child the behaviour you do want, and which will be rewarded.

■ A sanction will only work if the child does not want to receive it.

■ Different sanctions will work best at different ages.

■ Different sanctions will work best for different types of children.

■ Different sanctions will work best for you as a parent, for instance in terms of the effort they take to apply.

■ Find out as quickly as you can which sanctions work best for you and your children and use them.

■ Remember that children are constantly changing, and what works well one day might not work at all the next.

■ If you threaten a sanction, you must deliver it, otherwise you will undermine your authority.

■ If a sanction is given, the child must serve it, or it has no meaning. The message you send if you don't follow through is that your threats are empty ones.

■ If your child believes that she won't have to serve the sanction, then she will also realize that she doesn't have to do what you ask.

■ Using sanctions clearly and consistently will allow you to use them less, because your child will know that you mean what you say.

■ Try to be fair – don't give a heavier punishment than the behaviour deserves.

■ Be very clear about what's going on. State what the misbehaviour is, why the sanction has been earned, what it will be, and when your child will serve it.

■ Learn to keep your emotions out of it – if you are wound up or angry, you will not be able to deal with the problem fairly and rationally.

■ Try to keep the situation depersonalized if possible, blaming the behaviour rather than the child.

■ Do remember to be flexible – let the child 'win back' sometimes, when the situation merits it, or when you feel you might have been unfair. Make it clear to the child that this is what you are doing.

■ The best and most effective sanctions are free and easy to use. For a child who respects and loves her parents, your displeasure or disapproval sends a very powerful message.

Instant v deferred sanctions

As with rewards, as your child gets older you will be able to use some deferred sanctions. Remember, though, that much of the power of punishment is in the instant connection between the poor behaviour and its consequences. Threatening a child that 'when your father gets home he's going to sort you out' is rather vague. In fact, by the time the father returns, the child may well have forgotten exactly what the misbehaviour was.

Of course, these deferred punishments may send a message in that they leave your child to stew over the misbehaviour. On the whole, though, the sooner you can administer the sanction, the better it will be. There really is no point in either of you dwelling on misbehaviour – once it has happened, hand out the sanction, get it served and then move on to more positive things.

Types of sanctions

Your disapproval

- This is one of the most powerful sanctions of all.
- It's especially useful where the parents have a strong partnership with their children.
- This sanction is free and easy to use.
- Try to match your level of disapproval with how 'bad' you believe the misbehaviour to be.
- Be disappointed rather than angry, it's much more effective.

Shouting

- Shouting is not especially effective as a sanction.
- It is free, but using it puts stress on you personally.
- Shouting can exacerbate a situation where a child is getting out of control.
- A good tip is to shout when you're not actually angry – that way you keep control of yourself and your emotions.
- See the section on pp. 107–9 for more thoughts about shouting.

Removal

- Removal is straightforward and relatively easy to use.
- It separates you and your child when stress levels are likely to be high for you both.
- You might be removing the child from the room, putting her somewhere safe.
- You could be removing an object from the child, if she cannot handle it properly, or looks likely to damage it.

- You might be removing a toy from the child, or privileges, such as time on the computer.
- You could simply be removing your attention from the child.

Loss of privileges

- Taking privileges away from your child is free and relatively easy to do.
- Make sure that certain areas are seen as a privilege rather than a right.
- This might include watching TV, going to bed later than usual, and so on.
- Look at the section on rights and responsibilities (pp. 71–75) for more thoughts about this.

The 'naughty' place

- This sanction involves designating a specific place for the child to go when she has misbehaved.
- It is similar to the idea of 'removal' described above.
- You might use the bottom step, or perhaps a particular stool or seat.
- The 'naughty' place 'stands for' your disapproval.
- Having to sit still for a length of time gives your child a chance to think about what she's done.
- This sanction will only work if your child actually sits where she's told and does not move.

How to give sanctions

You might think that giving sanctions is as simple as just saying what the punishment is, and making sure that your child serves it. However, the sanctions that you give will actually be more effective if you can learn to apply them in the right way. By giving sanctions correctly, you will mini-mize the negative effects that can result when you have to use punishment. Here are some tips to show you how to do this:

■ Before you start, get close to your child, rather than shouting across the room. Keep the giving of sanctions as private as you can.

■ This is particularly important when you have more than one child – you don't want any siblings to act as an audi-ence and consequently to raise the stakes for the child being punished.

■ Get down on her level, for instance sitting beside her on the floor.

■ Make sure that she is looking at you, focused on what you're going to say.

■ Use your child's name to get her attention, and try to get her making eye contact with you.

■ Make sure that you are feeling calm and cool before you start – don't allow your child's misbehaviour to get you riled or you won't deal with the situation in a rational way.

■ If the situation merits, try distracting your child from her misbehaviour, rather than applying sanctions immediately.

■ This might involve suggesting a positive alternative behaviour.

■ If the misbehaviour is serious enough to need dealing with immediately, state what the poor behaviour is, and why it is not allowed.

■ Tell your child whether you are going to sanction her immediately, or whether you will only need to sanction if she does not discontinue the misbehaviour.

■ Make it very clear what the sanction for this mis-behaviour (or for continuing it) will be.

■ If your child is too young to understand, give her signals through your tone of voice and your face.

■ Apply the sanction in as calm and firm a way as you possibly can.

■ Ensure that your child serves the sanction. Remember, if you don't follow through your initial threat will be seen as meaningless.

What about smacking?

The issue of smacking does seem to bring out very strong emotions in people, either completely for or firmly against the whole idea. Before I go any further, let me say that I understand completely why you might smack your child. However, it's my opinion that smacking doesn't work as a control strategy. My belief is that the only person that smacking might 'work' for is the parent, perhaps because it allows you to blow off steam or to feel more in control of your child when nothing else is working.

It's my opinion, and you may well not agree, that smacking is wrong. My feeling is that it is not right to use physical approaches to dominate another person, especially when that person is smaller than you. We would never dream of hitting a fellow office worker if he or she wasn't doing what we wanted. It surely follows that we have no right to hit our children, whatever the provocation?

As a teacher, I am not allowed to use physical violence against my students, no matter what they do to me (and I have been sworn at and threatened with physical attack on several occasions). The so-called 'good old days', where the cane or a smack with a ruler was permitted are long gone. To my mind, this is a very good thing.

Having said all this, I do understand some of the reasons why you might use the occasional smack to discipline your child. Below I've put the case for both sides of the argument. It is then up to you to make up your own mind about whether or not to use smacking as a form of punishment with your child.

Smacking: for and against

Why smack?
■ It provides a short, sharp shock.

- It can be used as a way of signalling extreme disapproval.
- It can be used to indicate when something is very dangerous.
- It can sometimes solve a behaviour issue instantly.

Why not smack?

- It can be over-used for minor misbehaviours that would be better controlled in other ways.
- It can lead to attention-seeking, where the child misbehaves to gain the 'attention' of a physical contact with the parent (even though this is a smack).
- If used to discipline a child who is simply exploring her world, it might put her off this valuable learning experience.
- Adults are big, children are small – is physical dominance really appropriate?
- It sends the message that hitting others is acceptable, and may lead to the child experimenting with violence against others, for instance siblings.
- If the adult loses control of his or her temper, it could be that a single smack might lead to something more serious.

Positive praise, positive punishment: the plan

As soon as your child is old enough to understand, you might like to introduce a more specific way of noting good behaviour and discouraging misbehaviour. This could be particularly useful if you are experiencing more severe difficulties with your child, although it will work just as well for the child who normally behaves well. The idea is to start making positive behaviours more concrete – to find a way of recording them visually or physically so that your child knows what she is aiming for. Creating a plan in this way will also help you to develop the use of deferred gratification.

The plan that I give below offers you one way of introducing a scheme for getting the behaviour that you want. As you'll see, it focuses strongly on rewarding the right behaviours, rather than on noting the wrong ones. The key is to encourage the behaviour you do want, rather than the behaviour that you don't. You can do this by setting your child the targets that you want her to achieve. The instructions below will help you to set up the plan and to adapt it to suit your own needs. I have then given an example of one possible plan to show you how it works.

- Create a chart to go on the wall. If your child is old enough, it's a great idea to work together with her to make the chart.

- Note: you can actually buy charts in children's shops, although it's my feeling that a homemade one will probably be more attractive and fun.

- Divide the chart into columns, one for each type of positive behaviour.

- Label each column at the bottom with the behaviour that you want.

- You might use very specific behaviours that you are trying to encourage, for instance 'going to bed at 7pm'. You might use more generalized targets, such as 'getting dressed properly' and so on.

- Remember that the more visually attractive your chart is, the more likely your child is to respond positively to it. For instance, this could mean using coloured paper or felt pens to draw animals, etc. on the chart.

- Find some way of recording each incidence of positive behaviour, for instance with a gold star or other sticker.

- Decide on how many stars your child must achieve before she receives a 'big' reward. This might be watching extra TV, receiving pocket money or any other reward that works for you.

- Note: for some children, simply receiving the stars will be enough; for others you will need to work towards a bigger reward.

- Put the chart on the wall in a prominent place, somewhere that you can easily refer to it. This might be beside your child's chair or in her bedroom.

- Talk through the plan with your child, making it clear what she must do to earn her stickers.

- For each positive behaviour, she will earn one sticker to go on the chart.

- When she does achieve a positive behaviour, it is a good idea to let your child put the sticker on the chart for herself. This will help her feel that she 'owns' the plan.

- As an alternative to the chart, you might like to use another approach, for instance putting marbles in a jar.

Sample plan for positive praise, positive punishment

BEHAVIOURS								NUMBER OF STICKERS
Getting dressed properly	Getting ready for school on time	Doing your homework	Eating all your dinner	Sharing toys with sister	Cleaning your teeth	Going to bed on time	Staying in bed all night	

EIGHT

Case Studies

Of course, the advice that I give in this book will only be useful if you can actually put it into practice in your own home. I have tried to make the tips and strategies that I offer as realistic and practical as possible, using my own experience as both a teacher and a mother. It can be helpful, though, to have some more specific information about what you might actually do in certain situations. In this chapter you will find some examples of problems that you might face with your children. For each of the case studies that I offer, I give details of:

- what the problem is
- why it might be happening, and
- what you can actually do to solve it

Do bear in mind that there is never one single answer when it comes to dealing with behaviour. So much will depend on the individual child, your style as a parent, your home situation and so on. To my mind, the keys to getting it right are the ability to be flexible and the willingness to keep trying different ideas until you find the ones that work for you.

Some of the problems that I deal with here are relatively minor, and hopefully quite easy to solve. Some of the case studies deal with more serious issues, and it could be that you need to turn to outside professionals for advice and help.

The attention-seeking child

What's the problem?

- Frequent low-level misbehaviour, designed to attract your attention.
- Highly irritating, but not really a serious issue (although it can develop into one if not dealt with).
- Examples might include:
  - throwing toys to make you say 'no!'
  - running away from you in the supermarket so that you are forced to chase
- Lots of whingeing when he doesn't get his own way.
- Looking at you immediately after misbehaviour to check your reaction, effectively to say 'look how naughty I'm being'.

Why is it happening?

- Too much focus given to poor behaviour, for instance making a big deal out of low-level misbehaviour that doesn't really merit it.
- Not understanding that attention is a powerful reward to a child.
- Not understanding that even disapproval, smacking or shouting are still forms of reward, because it means the parent is taking notice.
- Failing to offer enough attention when the child is going the right thing, ignoring the child rather than making approval clear.
- Over time the child gets the message that, to get the reward of attention, he should misbehave.

- This eventually becomes a habit that will need to be broken.

- Bear in mind that, just as the initial message took time to sink in, so breaking the habit will take time as well.

- Note: if the attention-seeking behaviour is extreme, and does not seem to get better after a long period of time, then a medical issue could be involved and help should be sought.

What can I do about it?

- Try using distraction whenever possible, rather than giving your attention for negative behaviours.

- Look for the positive things that your child does – force yourself to focus on these as much as you possibly can.

- When your child does something right, offer lots of verbal praise and perhaps bigger, more concrete rewards too.

- You might use the plan described on p. 133 to reinforce the behaviour that you want.

- Using this chart will also help remind you to give your attention for the right behaviours.

- Try as hard as possible not to give your attention for minor misbehaviours.

- Bear in mind that you are breaking a habit too! It could take a while for you to change your focus.

- Only use sanctions when you really feel the behaviour merits them.

- Use the 'tactical ignore' (see pp. 115–6 for details of this).

- Remember that you will need to stick with these approaches for a while before you can expect to see results.

- Above all else, don't give in if these strategies don't work immediately – give them time and you will see a difference.

The child who can't concentrate

What's the problem?

- Inability to focus on one activity at a time.
- Unable to sit still for long periods, without making a fuss.
- Playing with one toy for only seconds, before discarding it and moving onto something else.
- Finding it hard to pay attention to what people are saying, whether parents, other adults or children.
- May also be combined with generally slower development, for instance in reading or manual dexterity.

Why is it happening?

- The child might never have been 'trained' in how to concentrate, or expected to concentrate for long periods of time.
- Too many toys might have been given at once, without the child being shown how to play with any one thing in a focused way.
- Excessive use of TV/video games: these can over-stimulate a child so that he needs similar levels of stimulation to maintain his attention.
- Age will have an impact – better concentration will develop as a child grows older.
- Additives or substances in food and drink can also cause problems with concentration.

What can I do about it?

- Limit your child's access to TV and video games – make these a reward rather than a right.
- Get your child playing games which encourage extended periods of concentration, for instance cards, Connect 4 or building bricks.
- If you have more than one child, you could encourage them to play these games together, perhaps asking an older child to help a younger sibling.

- Teach your child some exercises that require concentration, such as mental arithmetic or spelling his name backwards in his head.

- Encourage calm, still and focused activities that require your child to sit still.

- Set time targets, for instance 10 minutes, concentrated focus on his homework, then reward your child when he does maintain his focus for this period of time.

- Read books with your child: not only will this develop his concentration, but it also plays a vital role in helping him learn to read and write well. In addition it gives you a wonderful chance to bond with each other. Again, if you have older children you might ask them to take on this adult task for you, to encourage closer bonds between them.

The destructive child

What's the problem?

- Destructive behaviour with the child's belongings, such as tearing books or throwing toys.

- Destructive behaviour with your belongings, for instance shoving objects into the video machine slot.

- 'Vandalizing' things around the home, perhaps scribbling on the walls or damaging the furniture.

- Trashing his room for no apparent reason.

Why is it happening?

- A certain amount of destructive behaviour is an entirely natural part of growing up, although it should diminish as your child gets older.

- Seeing how things can be taken apart or manipulated helps your child to learn about the world.

- In some circumstances we might allow destructive behaviour, for instance knocking down towers of blocks or tearing up paper.

■ In some situations we will not allow this behaviour, for example where the object is expensive or fragile.

■ Right from the start the child is learning what is and isn't allowed by his parents.

■ If the signals sent are not clear, or the expectations not consistent, then confusion and boundary testing will probably occur.

■ Lack of early training in how to respect his belongings and his environment.

■ Some children do naturally seem to have more destructive personalities than others.

What can I do about it?

■ Try to set very clear expectations right from the start about what is and is not allowed.

■ If you have allowed these behaviours in the past, then take some time to explain why you are now going to clamp down on them.

■ Keep your expectations clear and consistent – always react in the same way to the same destructive behaviours.

■ Use positive approaches as often as possible, making a big deal when your child demonstrates constructive behaviour.

■ For instance this might mean praising your child when he helps you to clear up or when he tidies his room.

■ Trying to distract your child from destructive actions by offering a positive alternative.

■ Applying sanctions in a clear and firm way when the destructive behaviour does occur.

■ If your child seems to have a naturally destructive personality, you might allow him to let this out by giving him some paper or other unimportant things to tear up.

■ Setting up some destructive learning activities for two siblings, for instance getting each of them to build robots in the style of the TV programme 'Robot Wars' and then having a 'war' between the two.

■ Keeping temptation out of the way to make your life easier.

The seriously disruptive child

What's the problem?

- Extreme examples of poor behaviour, such as physical or verbal abuse or aggression, directed either at the parents, siblings or at other people outside the home.
- Tantrums that do not seem to lessen with age or to respond to the techniques outlined in this book.
- A child who seems unable to control his impulses.
- A child who gets wound up and angry over minor things.
- Serious misbehaviour outside the home, for instance when he starts school.

Why is it happening?

- Lack of boundaries and clear expectations right from the start.
- Confusion over what misbehaviour is, and what the consequences of misbehaving will be.
- Extreme example of attention-seeking behaviour.
- Negative approaches used far more than positive ones.
- Confrontational approaches used by the parent, rather than a calm and considered attitude.
- Lack of flexibility in the parenting style – seeing behaviour as a 'win or lose' scenario and consequently raising the stakes.
- Getting into a negative frame of mind, where the parent starts to expect poor behaviour, and immediately becomes defensive when misbehaviour occurs.
- There might be an external reason for this behaviour – for instance if there are problems in the parents' relationship this can sometimes lead to the child 'acting up' in a serious way.
- Sometimes this type of behaviour can indicate a specific behavioural problem that might have medical grounds.

What can I do about it?

- Make sure that you get the problem sorted as soon as possible.

- This type of behaviour can cause all sorts of problems once your child starts at school, and has to understand for himself how to conform to the rules.

- Above all, aim to focus on the positive. Read this book from cover to cover, and try to put as many of the strategies into place as you can.

- When your child does lose control, take a moment to step back from the situation before you deal with it.

- Take a calm, controlled approach – never allow poor behaviour to wind you up, as this will encourage it to be repeated.

- Don't expect instant results – bad habits quickly become ingrained, and it takes time for good habits to replace them.

- Don't blame yourself – we all make mistakes, it's making the effort to put things right that is important.

- If you're at all worried, get your child checked out by the professionals: he might have a specific special need that has not yet been identified, such as ADHD (Attention Deficit Hyperactivity Disorder).

- Don't try to cope alone – get help from advisory agencies or simply talk to other parents who are going through the same thing as you.

Sibling rivalry

What's the problem?

- Poor relationship between siblings.
- Physical or verbal attacks on each other: scratching, biting, arguing and so on.
- Refusal to cooperate, for instance by sharing toys or playing together.
- Winding each other up at every opportunity, particularly

where it is difficult for the parents to intervene, for instance in the car or when out at the shops.

Why is it happening?

- A certain amount of friction is entirely natural and normal.
- Children with different personalities might wind each other up.
- The older child may experience jealousy when his place as the 'baby' is taken away from him.
- It could be that the parents have given more attention to the new child, probably without realizing what they are doing.
- This is hard for the first child to deal with: his natural reaction is to blame the baby for taking his parents' attention away.
- Consequently, he decides to get attention by being naughty, or takes out his frustration on his younger sibling.

What can I do about it?

- Before the new sibling arrives, talk to your child about what is going to happen. Obviously, he must be old enough to understand for this to work.
- Read some books together about brothers and sisters.
- Focus on the positive aspects of his new sibling – make it seem like an exciting challenge about to happen.
- Go out with your first child to buy a present for the new baby, and buy a present for your first child for the baby to 'give' him.
- When you bring the new baby home, make sure that you lavish attention on your first child as well as often as possible (and yes, I do know how tired you will be!).
- Spend quality time with each child as an individual as much as you possibly can.
- Refuse to be distracted when you are playing with one child by misbehaviour or attention seeking from the other child.

- Make getting on well together a challenge for which your children can aim.

- Treat the older child as an 'adult' and encourage him to take care of/help out with the younger child.

- Don't get drawn into arguments about who did what. Set the boundaries and be firm about what you want.

- Don't expect miracles: accept that sometimes children will simply not get on with each other.

- Perhaps one child takes after his mother in personality, while the other takes after her father. It could be that the two different personality types simply don't mix.

NINE

Behaviour and School

In this chapter, I deal with your children's behaviour away from the home environment. This section focuses mainly on your child's formal years of school-based education. However, much of the advice that I give here will also be useful to those parents who have returned to work, and whose children have gone into paid childcare at an earlier age.

Children spend the first part of their lives mainly in the home, whether this is the first few months or the first few years. At this stage the child's parents meet her every need. You take care of her, you take responsibility for her, you make sure that she knows how she is supposed to behave. Then the day comes for her to start school (or nursery/at a child-minder), to move out into the big wide world on her own. Now is the time that she will start to have to take at least some responsibility for her own behaviour, in conjunction with the other adults who are helping to care for her. Of course, the level of personal responsibility for behaviour will clearly depend on the child's age, but by the time they start school most children are able to be reasonably independent in this area.

I'd like to start this chapter by reassuring you that generally speaking most children do behave well at school. This applies particularly where the school is well run, and where the approaches I have outlined in this book are put into practice as a way of managing behaviour, both by the parents and by the school. However, there will be some situations where misbehaviour does become a problem. For instance, where behaviour in the school is not well managed, or where a child does not have the strategies in place to take responsibility for her own behaviour.

There are plenty of things that you can do to help prepare your own child for starting at school. If you can put the strategies and ideas from this book into practice right from the start, you will ensure that your child has a good basis for knowing how to behave properly. In this chapter you can find some more specific ideas for how to influence your child's behaviour at school in a positive way. I also look at what you might do if things go wrong.

Home/school communication

Please do feel that you can approach your child's teacher or school (or nursery/childminder) if you are worried about something. I can promise you that the school really wants you to get involved with your child's education. Keeping the lines of communication between the home and the school open plays a really important part in ensuring that your child does her very best at school, especially when it comes to her behaviour.

If your child's teacher does have to tell you that your child has misbehaved, please don't get defensive. He or she will be trying to do the very best for your child, and this includes facing any problems head on. There are various ways in which you can communicate with your child's school. I have listed some of these in the section below.

Forms of contact

One of the most important ways of ensuring that your child behaves well is to keep in regular contact with the school. The physical divide between home and school can mean that children think that they can 'get away' with behaviour without their parents knowing. If your child sees that you know what's going on during the school day, she is less likely to try it on. You can also be given information about ways of supporting the teacher, for instance working together to set behaviour targets for your child.

There are various different ways of keeping in contact with your child's school and these include:

- *In person* Some schools encourage parents to talk to their child's teacher at the start or end of the school day. When your child first starts school, you will obviously want to go in with her to settle her into the class. You might also have a quick word with the teacher at this point to check how she's getting on. Do bear in mind, though, that teachers are very busy people who have a whole class of children. Please understand if your child's school prefers you to make a formal appointment to discuss any concerns you might have.

- *By telephone* If you're happy for the school to phone you, then tell the teacher that he or she can get in touch whenever necessary. Often the suggestion that the teacher might phone home is enough to ensure good behaviour. If the child knows that her teacher is willing to get in touch with her parents, she is far less likely to feel like she can get away with poor behaviour.

- *Through diaries* Many schools now use a diary system, whereby the children have a diary in which their teachers can write notes to the home. If this is the case for your child, then have a look through this diary as soon as your child starts school. Find out where rewards such as merit marks are written, and make it clear to your child that you will be looking for these positive signs. Check also to see where detentions or other sanctions are recorded in case your child does misbehave.

- *In reports* About once every term, your child will receive a detailed report about how she is getting on at school. This report will tell you all about her progress in her learning, but it will also be a place where her teacher can flag up any behaviour problems. If you do see the early signs of problems, for instance a comment that your child 'finds it hard to maintain her concentration', then get in touch with the teacher to discuss things further.

■ *At parents' meetings* The parents' meeting provides a formal setting in which you can discuss your child's progress. Sometimes these meetings take place in the evening after school; sometimes they are scheduled during the school day. It really is a very good idea to attend these meetings, preferably with your child in tow. In fact, speaking as a teacher, it is my experience that the parents who do attend are those who really care about their child's education, and whose children do tend to behave better. Don't be scared to ask lots of questions – if you have any concerns at all about your child's behaviour, the parents' meeting is a good time to ask. You might also set some targets with your child and her teacher so that she has something specific for which to aim.

■ *Getting involved* Of course, one of the very best ways that you can ensure good school/home communication is to get closely involved with your child's school. This might mean offering to help out in the classroom (your child's or another one), perhaps reading with individual children. Depending on your talents, you might offer to run an extra-curricular club for the school, for instance a computer or football club. You could become a parent governor or join the PTA (Parent Teacher Association). Being 'on the spot' like this will mean that you can keep an 'ear to the ground' for any signs of trouble.

How schools manage behaviour

Schools deal with the whole spectrum of behaviour: from children who are perfectly behaved and highly motivated, to those who bring very serious behaviour issues with them. There are various ways in which schools aim to manage behaviour. First and foremost, the teachers will be using many of the ideas that I have outlined in this book. They will be aiming to have high expectations and to set clear boundaries, to take positive approaches such as using rewards whenever possible, and also applying sanctions when necessary.

Schools also have more formalized approaches to dealing with behaviour, and some of these are listed below. It's a great idea for parents to understand what goes on at schools when it comes to managing behaviour, so that you can support the work that the teachers do with your child.

Whole-school behaviour policies

The majority of schools now have what is called a 'Whole-school behaviour policy'. This is a document that sets out in writing what the school wants from your child when it comes to her behaviour. Many schools will send parents an abbreviated copy of this document, perhaps in the form of the 'school rules'.

It really is worth getting to know the school behaviour policy that is used at your child's school. If you do, you can support the work that your child's school is doing. For instance, if your child comes home complaining about having received a sanction, you can discuss the misbehaviour, why it broke the school rules, and what the punishment was. On a more positive note, the school behaviour policy will list the rewards available, and you might also set your child targets for winning these rewards.

Home/school contracts

Schools are always keen for parents to be involved, particularly when it comes to managing behaviour. When parents work well with us as teachers, this inevitably has a positive impact on a child's behaviour. Home/school contracts are a great way for the school to formalize this partnership. A contract is drawn up by the school, which outlines the ways in which your child will be expected to behave. This contract is signed by the parents (and probably the child as well), to say that you agree to follow these rules.

Rewards and sanctions

Your child's school will focus mainly on the use of rewards, particularly with the youngest children. The aim is to encourage good behaviour by using positive reinforcement – catching the children being good and making sure it is rewarded. Typical school rewards might include:

- verbal praise
- stars and stickers
- merits or commendations
- certificates
- letters or phone calls home
- material rewards, such as sweets

Sometimes your child's teachers will have to turn to the use of sanctions. For instance, when dealing with serious misbehaviour, or simply with repeated low-level misbehaviour that does not respond to the use of rewards. The teacher's aim will always be to start at the lowest level of sanction, rather than jumping straight in with a high-level punishment. Typical sanctions at school might be:

- verbal reprimands
- a 'deadly' stare
- loss of privileges
- detentions
- being put 'on report'
- letters or phone calls home

Special needs

Some children do have more severe problems at school, either with their learning or with their behaviour. When this happens, teachers refer to a child as having 'SEN', an abbreviation for the term 'special educational needs'. Some children are born with these needs: for instance the child who is dyslexic or who has Down syndrome. In other instances, the child's upbringing might have contributed to the special needs, perhaps with some of the behavioural problems that we come across.

If it is thought that your child might have special needs, then the school will make contact with you to discuss what is happening. When the special needs are very high level, your child might be given a 'statement' that lists what her needs are and what is going to be done about them.

Some of the abbreviations that you might come across that relate specifically to behaviour problems include:

- *EBD*: emotional/behavioural disorder
- *ADD*: attention-deficit disorder
- *ADHD*: attention-deficit hyperactivity disorder

Choosing a nursery/school

Although in theory parents are supposed to have a choice of the school that their children attend, in reality this is often not the case. The 'best' schools will tend to be over-subscribed, receiving many more requests for places than they have space to offer. When paying for childcare at a nursery, the parents will obviously have greater choice over which one they choose, although again many of the best nurseries will not have places available. If you do have the chance to make a choice of nursery or school, look out for the following 'good signs' to help you find the best environment for your child:

- *Staff* Focus above all else on the children's welfare and happiness; lots of smiles and welcoming faces; clear expectations of positive behaviour; willing to spend time talking with parents about any questions or concerns.
- *Students* Seem happy and contented; polite and helpful to adults and other children; seem engaged and interested in learning.
- *Environment* Colourful and well-maintained displays; tidy and well-organized classrooms; no signs of vandalism; in a nursery, area for younger children to nap.
- *Educational opportunities* Plenty of different areas for learning; good balance of academic (literacy, numeracy)

and chances for more creative activities (art, music); opportunities for learning through play (water, sand, etc.); outdoor activities; lots of extra-curricular clubs and events.

- *Communication with parents* Good systems for keeping in touch with parents; willing for parents to raise any issues; high-quality reporting methods.

- *Break times* Good-quality lunches served; clean and well-organized area for eating; access to outdoors for play; playtimes well supervised by staff.

- *Ofsted reports* Schools and nurseries are inspected by a government organization called Ofsted (The Office for Standards in Education). This organization keeps a check on the educational and other standards in schools. If you have access to the internet, you can find the report for your local school at www.ofsted.gov.uk. Alternatively, you could ask your school for a copy of their most recent report.

Preparing for primary school

Starting at primary school can be an extremely stressful experience for our children (and for their poor parents as well!). This is especially so for the child who hasn't spent much time outside the home before. Those children who have been to nursery will probably find it easier, but you might still experience some difficulties. Bear in mind that school is a more formal environment than nursery, and that there will be a large number of children in your child's class, all demanding some of the teacher's attention.

As a teacher and a parent, I can hopefully give you some very useful tips here that will help you prepare your own child for primary school (and in addition make you very popular with your child's new teacher). You will help both your child and her teacher a great deal if your child has some knowledge or ability in the following areas:

- *Personal grooming* No teacher wants a whole class of children who cannot do the most basic things for themselves! Make sure that your child can dress herself, and preferably also tie her shoelaces. If this is too difficult for her as yet, then make sure that she wears shoes that don't have laces. For the nursery-age child, taking care of personal grooming might simply mean ensuring that you pack a spare set of clothes in the child's bag in case any accidents or messes occur.

■ *Personal hygiene* By the age of 5, it is hoped that most children will be able to go to the toilet by themselves. Make sure your child knows that she should ask if she does need the toilet, rather than waiting until it is too late, and having an accident.

■ *Personal belongings* Many behaviour problems in the school are caused by problems over personal belongings. If you send your child into school with an expensive toy or mobile phone, then don't be surprised if this causes problems. Keep your child's personal belongings to a minimum, focusing on the equipment that she needs for learning. Similarly, nurseries usually ask that children do not bring in their own toys from home (although a 'comforter' such as a cuddly toy might be exempt from this). By doing this, the nursery is simply trying to pre-empt any problems about lost items.

■ *Communication* Make sure that your child knows how to communicate with her teacher when she wants something. Some children are scared of their teachers – you can help by explaining that the teacher only wants the best for her. You can also help your child by telling her that the teacher might be busy, and won't necessarily be able to deal with her immediately.

■ *Interaction* It's important that your child is able to interact properly with other children. By the age of 4 or 5, she should have learned how to play cooperatively, how to share, and so on. If she cannot get on with others without arguments, she may get into trouble once she starts school. For younger children, who may not yet have these social skills, the nursery provides a great environment for starting to learn how to share.

■ *Social skills* Your child also needs to know how to make friends. If she is lucky, some of her friends might also go to the same school as her, and this will naturally help ease her into the situation. However, you will not be there to help her develop her socialization. Lay the groundwork for this by ensuring that she learns to mix early on, and that she has a good sense of empathy with others.

■ *Understands boundaries* If your child is brought up with a good idea of what boundaries are, and why she needs to stick to them, then she will find the 'school rules' easy to follow.

■ *Understands the use of rewards and sanctions* If you have already been using rewards and sanctions with your child at home, it should not prove too confusing for her when she starts at school. There are various rewards and sanctions that are commonly used in school. Make sure you know what these are, and why they might be given, so you can keep an eye on your child's progress both in behaviour and in learning.

Problems in the primary school

Schools are very busy places. Sometimes you might need to become a bit of a 'pushy parent' in order to get the best for your child. If you suspect that your child is having problems that are not being properly dealt with, then do get in touch with the school and insist that something is done. This might mean having a meeting with your child's teacher and perhaps a manager at the school to resolve the issue.

On the other hand, you do need to accept that your child will eventually have to learn to fend for herself. Be careful only to intervene when it seems like the problem is not going to be resolved without your help, or when the issue seems a particularly serious one. Below you can find some tips on what to do in two particular situations that you might come across when your child starts school.

Bullying

It's inevitable that, when large groups of children are put together in an enclosed environment, some bullying will occur. Often, bullying is about jealousy – a child who works and behaves well, and who is praised a lot, might encounter jealous reactions from her peers. Most schools have very clear guidelines about bullying, and about what will happen to resolve the problem. Bullying takes many forms, from the lowest level of name calling, to much more serious issues such as physical attacks.

Some children will quickly turn to adults when they feel that they are being picked on, others will keep the problem to themselves for fear of things getting worse. As a parent, you will need to decide when your intervention is going to help, and when it might simply exacerbate the situation. Clearly, if the problem is serious and you feel that the school is not sorting it out, then you will have to step in to get things resolved. When this is the case, you might approach the head teacher or even the school's governing body to raise your concerns.

Here is some advice for dealing with the problem of bullying, both tips that you can give your child, and also what you can do about it yourself:

■ *Keep an eye out for the 'symptoms'* Sometimes the child will be too scared to report bullying. Keep a watch on your child and talk to her regularly about what happens at school. If you notice that she is becoming withdrawn, or seems to be scared about going to school, then it could be that there is some bullying going on.

■ *Just ignore it?* If the problem is low-level, for instance name calling, then you might advise your child to ignore the bullies. Most bullies are aiming to wind up their victims; to get a response of some sort. If your child can learn simply to rise above it, and not give them the reinforcement or reaction that they seek, then hopefully the bullies will stop of their own accord.

■ *Don't keep it to yourselves* If your child is being more seriously affected by bullying, then encourage her to tell her teacher what is going on, or contact the school yourself if you have concerns. The school should have some sort of structure in place to deal with bullying. The problem with involving 'authority' is that it can escalate rather than solve the bullying, because it raises the stakes for both sides. You will need to tread carefully, although of course you should never be afraid to step in when necessary.

- *Access a bullying programme* Ask the school if they run a bullying programme of some sort. This might involve the use of 'peer mentors', children who step in to talk with the two parties involved to try and resolve things between them. These peer-group programmes work well because they encourage the children to solve any issues for themselves. If your school does not have a programme already in place, then why not suggest that they should set one up?

- *Not just in the classroom* Often bullying will take place in the playground, or perhaps on the journey to or from school, where there is less chance for adults to intervene. Make sure that your child knows the right person to turn to – in the playground there will be supervisors available who can keep an eye on her.

- *Try to see both sides* There are always two sides to every situation. Although it is tempting as a parent to immediately side with your child, and to jump in and try to help out, it is worth taking the time to find out what is really going on. Could it be that your child is winding up the other children in some way, and that they are simply responding to this, rather than actually bullying her? If you do feel that these are genuine bullies, then it is still worth trying to see things from their side, even if this just means feeling sorry for them because they have not been brought up properly or had good parents from whom to learn how to behave.

Poor teacher/child relationships

Teachers are only human, and sometimes you will come across a situation where your child simply does not get on with her teacher, and perhaps vice versa. At primary school, where your child will have the same teacher for the whole year, this is a problem that needs solving. Your child might come home complaining that she 'hates' her teacher, or that her teacher is picking on her. Here are some tips about what to do in this situation:

- *Listen to her* Make time to listen to your child's complaints. Sometimes all a child needs is a sympathetic ear, or a shoulder to cry on. It could be that once she has been able to share her concerns with you, and to get the problem out in the open, it seems less important than she at first imagined.

- *Reason with her* Once you have let her 'get it all out', then it's time to explore the situation rationally. If you actually ask your child what has happened, you might realize that in fact all the teacher did was sanction misbehaviour in a perfectly justified way. If this is the case you can talk to your child about why her behaviour was wrong, and why the sanctions were deserved.

- *Support the teacher* Although I know it's hard, I would generally advise against taking your child's side in this sort of situation. Although you might have some sympathy with her point of view, you will not be doing her any favours if you undermine her teacher's authority. It is often the case that when a child accuses a teacher of picking on her, this is actually the teacher simply laying down the law. Bear in mind that it is very rare that children are actually able to change classes and teachers – many primary schools will only have one class in each year group.

- *Accept that the teacher is human* Sometimes even we teachers make mistakes! It could be that, in the hustle and bustle of the classroom situation, the teacher has indeed been unfair to your child. It's inevitable that teachers will get things wrong sometimes, although hopefully this won't happen too often. Although to the child involved this might seem like a terrible injustice, in fact it's all part of school life.

- *Learn to live with it* Your child will need to learn to live with situations that aren't entirely fair – it's a fact of life that we must all eventually accept. By helping your child understand this, you will help her to deal with the problem in a mature way.

- *If necessary, have a word with the teacher or take it higher* If you do feel that the above advice is not applicable in your child's particular situation, then why not contact the teacher and have a chat. The teacher might not be aware of your child's feelings, and a quick word could be all that is needed to set things straight. Alternatively, if you feel that the issue has gone beyond a simple chat with the class teacher, then you are perfectly entitled to contact a more senior member of staff at your child's school. Ask whether you can meet with the head teacher or a deputy head to discuss your concerns.

Preparing for secondary school

Although this book deals mainly with the ages from 0 to 11 years, before your child arrives at secondary school, the advice that I give here is certainly applicable to children of all ages. When it comes to preparing for secondary school, the brief advice below hopefully should help you in getting your child ready to make this move.

- *Understand that it's a big change* It's worth being aware of how big a change the move to secondary school is for your child. She will go from having one teacher for the majority of her lessons, to having a different teacher for each one. She will also probably go from a relatively small school, with a small number of children, to a large school with perhaps over a thousand students.

- *Help her with the practicalities* There are various practical ways in which you can help your child during the first few weeks at school. Getting these areas right will mean that your child can concentrate on settling down and doing her work, rather than feeling worried about where she should be or what she will need. These practicalities might include helping her:
  - get her equipment and bag ready for the next day
  - get all her homework done
  - understand her timetable, and which lessons she has on which days
  - see why her teachers use sanctions, such as detentions, for certain behaviours
  - learn how to find her way around the school, for instance you might go over the school map with her to pinpoint the key rooms

■ *Understand the role of the form tutor* While she was at primary school, your child's class teacher would have kept an eye on both her learning and her overall welfare. In the secondary school, the form tutor is responsible for the pastoral care of your child. This means that he or she will deal with any issues that are not related specifically to lessons and learning. This might be helping the Year 7 students to settle in, talking with them about any concerns, and so on. Your child's form tutor is the first person for her, and you, to turn to if things are not going as you might wish.

TEN

When Things Get Tough

The majority of childhood behaviour issues do sort themselves out in their own good time. There are very few sixteen-year-olds still having toddler-style temper tantrums (although parents of hormonal teens might disagree!). If you apply the ideas and strategies that I've outlined in this book hopefully you should be able to deal with the majority of behaviour problems that you face. However, I do fully accept that there will be times when your child or children's behaviour gets on top of you, or when you face issues that seem just too big to solve alone.

In this final chapter, I give some ideas and information about what you can do when things get really tough. I look at how you can examine your own behaviour-management approaches, to see whether you can adapt the ways you work with your children to help yourself manage them better. I give some key 'coping strategies' for you to try, to deal with stress and that overwhelming feeling that everything is out of control. I also give you a directory listing sources of advice and support – organizations to which you can turn when your problems seem insurmountable.

Learning to self-evaluate

When things are going really badly wrong, the ability to evaluate and examine your own behaviour management is a vital part of making changes for the better. Over the years as a teacher, I've come across a number of situations where I simply could not get control of a class's behaviour. At these points in my career I had two basic choices: I could either just give up and wait for the end of the school year (not an option for parents), or I could look at myself and my practice closely to see what I could change to improve the situation.

At this point I'd like to make it clear that I am definitely not suggesting that you sit down and criticize yourself about all the things you are doing wrong. Instead, I want to help you look at yourself in a more reflective way, so that you have more chance of coping when things do get really tough. The idea is not to establish who is to 'blame' for a behaviour problem, but rather to see whether things could be done better in the future. As well as looking for what went wrong, I also ask you to examine what you did well in these circumstances, so that you might repeat this in the future.

When you do have a 'run-in' with your child, after the situation is over and things have calmed down, it is well worth taking some time to consider what happened. Being able to do this hopefully will help prevent you making the same mistakes in the future. Below I've put a list of questions that you might ask yourself, in an attempt to find out where things went wrong, and how you might improve them for the better.

Questions for self-evaluation

- How, why and when did the situation first start? (Many times the key lies here – what escalates into a major incident often begins in a very trivial way.)

- Were external factors affecting the situation – was my child in a bad mood, had a bad day at school, stressed about something, etc.? If these were involved, bear in mind that you have little chance of affecting these areas.
- Could I have distracted or re-directed my child to prevent us getting into a confrontation?
- What exactly went wrong between me and my child?
- Did I do anything to make the situation worse? This might include:
  - not making it clear what I wanted
  - over-reacting to a minor incident
  - seeing the issue as 'win or lose'
  - backing my child into a corner
  - letting my emotions get in the way
  - being negative, rather than positive, in my approaches
  - using negative language, such as sarcasm
  - using immediate sanctions and punishments
  - shouting or losing my temper
- What did I do well in dealing with the situation? This might include:
  - trying my hardest to stay calm, despite provocation
  - being fair and reasonable
  - offering my child a 'way out', even though he didn't take it
  - not shouting, despite the fact that I felt like it
  - trying to focus on positive approaches, until there was no alternative but to sanction
- How could I deal with this type of situation better in the future?

Key coping strategies

Of course there will be times when evaluating yourself is the last thing you want to do. The key coping strategies that I give below are tips learnt from dealing with children's

behaviour over many years. In the classroom, I have sometimes faced really tough times, where a whole class of children seems intent on refusing to comply with me, or where
an individual student makes my life really hard. At least as a
teacher I have the knowledge that I will be going home at the
end of the day to comfort me: as a parent there is no escape
from our responsibilities, even when things get really
difficult.

The strategies given below have helped me cope with the
toughest of times in the classroom. I hope that they give you
some comfort and ideas for when you are going through a
really difficult patch with your own children.

- *Keep a perspective* When things are going badly wrong, it's
  very easy for us to lose our sense of perspective. Do try at
  all times to keep a sense of what's really important, and
  this will help you stay cool and unemotional. You will
  then be able to deal with misbehaviour in the best possible way. It really isn't the end of the world if your child
  does misbehave, even if the misbehaviour is serious and
  constant. Remember that all over the world there are
  parents who cannot even feed their children adequately –
  we are lucky that we have the luxury of worrying about
  behaviour.

- *Try to stay positive* As well as using positive approaches
  with your child, do try to stay positive with yourself.
  Look for what you're doing right, and this will help you
  cope. Even if your children are behaving horribly, there
  are bound to be some things that you're doing well. You
  might be succeeding in areas other than behaviour – for a
  start, if you get your children fed, dressed and into school
  every morning, then you should give yourself a pat on
  the back.

- *Don't be too hard on yourself* I have tried to reinforce this
  message throughout the book, because I'm well aware
  how difficult it is to keep up all these 'perfect' ideas that I
  give. Please don't be too hard on yourself if you find it
  impossible to stay positive sometimes, or if you feel right
  at the end of your tether. You will get it wrong sometimes,
  so accept this and don't beat yourself up about it. Instead,
  learn from your mistakes and try your hardest to get it

162

right next time. Remember that this is a process of learning for both you and your children.

- *Build a wall* Learn to build an invisible wall between yourself and your children's behaviour. Allow silliness, rudeness, or even aggression to bounce off this wall rather than letting it get to you. I'm not saying that it's okay for your child to treat you like this, but rather that you should try not to allow this type of behaviour to affect you and the way that you react.

- *Don't give up* Even if the ideas that I've given in this book don't seem to work at first, do keep trying. It will take lots of time for your children to learn how to behave, especially if you've not used similar strategies and approaches in the past.

- *Take small steps* Look on every small step as a success – the smallest positive change in your children's behaviour should be greeted with a sense of achievement. Eventually these small steps will add up together to make a better and happier family life.

- *Be willing to admit when you're wrong* We all make mistakes when dealing with our children. If you are willing to admit when you get it wrong, rather than pretending that you never make mistakes, you will find that your children probably respect you a lot more.

- *Make life easy on yourself* As often as you can, make life easy on yourself. I manage to keep on top of the washing, but I don't iron anything, unless I need a specific item for business. We don't need to be perfect homemakers – the priority is turning out children who are properly fed, cared for and well brought up.

- *Find support when you need it* There are many sources of support to whom you can turn when things are getting really difficult to bear – family, friends, play groups, parenting organizations, and so on. Don't be afraid to ask for help when you really can't cope anymore.

- *Devote some time to yourself* When times are really tough, it is tempting to put yourself at the back of the queue. This is a mistake. A little time devoted solely to your own physical and mental health could make all the difference between coping and not coping as a parent.

Directory

In this section you can find details of organizations offering support to parents and their children. Many of these organizations run helplines that you can phone for advice when you're at the end of your tether. I have included a brief description of what each organization offers, telephone contact details, and also website addresses for those parents with access to the internet.

National Family and Parenting Institute

Online database of parenting and family support services in England and Wales.
Website: www.nfpi.org.uk

National Children's Bureau

Organization promoting the interests and well-being of children.
Telephone: 020 7843 6000
Website: www.ncb.org.uk

Babycentre

Great website giving advice and information. Excellent 'birth clubs' where you can make contact with parents of children born at the same time as your own.
Website: www.babycentre.co.uk

E-parents

Website with some useful advice and links on behaviour-related issues.
www.e-parents.org

NSPCC (National Society for Prevention of Cruelty to Children)

Charity concerned with looking after the interests of children, and protecting them from abuse.

Telephone: 020 7825 2500
Website: www.nspcc.org.uk

Parent Line Plus

Support service for parents.

Helpline: 0808 800 2222
Website: www.parentlineplus.org.uk

One Parent Families

Organization giving advice, support and information to single-parent families.

Helpline: 0800 018 5026
Website: www.oneparentfamilies.org.uk

Multiple Births Foundation

Organization giving advice and help for parents of twins, triplets and other multiple-birth families.

Telephone: 020 8383 3519
Website: www.multiplebirths.org.uk

Bullying

Advice for parents and pupils.

Website: www.bullying.co.uk

Kidscape

National charity whose aims are to prevent bullying and child abuse.

Helpline: 08451 205204
Website: www.kidscape.org.uk

Anti Bullying Campaign (ABC)

Advice and support service with trained counsellors.
Helpline: 020 7378 1446

Independent Panel for Special Educational Advice

Organization giving advice for parents of children with special educational needs.
Helpline: 0800 0184016
Website: www.ipsea.org.uk

Education Otherwise

Support for parents who want to educate their children outside the mainstream school system.
Helpline: 0870 7300074
Website: www.education-otherwise.org.uk

Index